# BOOMER'S BEYOND EMOJIS

*Boomer's Guide to Navigate Challenging Digital Situations,
Reduce Embarrassing Misunderstandings, and Improve
Relationships with Your Grandkids*

## ALEXANDER VAUGHN

# CONTENTS

# INTRODUCTION

Did you know that globally, about three billion people have a social media account (*Top 50 Interesting Facts*, 2022)? Although we might tend to focus on the negative aspects of social media and new technologies, they actually improve our lives in many ways. If you have a child or a relative abroad, you've probably witnessed the incredible benefits of video calls that allow you to talk to and see everyone everywhere in the world. Thanks to these new digital tools, we can communicate easily, effectively, and rapidly, thus saving time and effort. However, keeping track of all of the changes is arduous, as new technologies are constantly developing, so you might feel like you live in a jungle with no clear path or accurate maps to navigate it.

How many times has your child or grandchild encouraged you to open yourself up to digital communication and try Facebook or Instagram? How do you feel about exploring the internet? On the one hand, you might want to build deeper connections with younger generations and try to use new social media and digital tools, while on the other hand, you might be afraid of doing things wrong or struggling to learn because the internet is a new, intricate world. At the same time, you might look at friends and people you know and be surprised by the way they manage to use the internet to their advantage, communicating with their children and grandchildren without problems. Encouraged by others' examples, you might have tried to download social media on your smartphone or to understand how online communication works, but then you might have felt disheartened by your results.

Well, if you have a problematic relationship with the online world, you're not the only one! Although some people manage to understand digital tools easily and use them as they want, only some have this expertise and savoir-faire! Like many people of your age, you might feel like you need more confidence to navigate the complexities of digital communication on your own to build a connection with younger generations, especially your grandchildren, who seem to know it all and have everything figured out. When you look at them, the internet seems easy to navigate, and all actions are natural and simple, but when you try, everything looks complicated and hard to decipher. At the same time, you might feel overwhelmed by all the rapid changes the digital landscape undergoes every month and year: One day, your grandchildren talk about Instagram, and the next one, they're all scrolling TikTok and posting videos online.

If you've tried to use social media on your own, you might have also noticed that conflict easily arises, and the way people communicate online is different from how they interact in the real world. Therefore, you might find it hard to comprehend all the nuances, use words and digital tools properly, and fear fostering negative interactions or engaging in unhealthy conversations when, in reality, you want the opposite. If you're not digitally literate, you might also worry about your own safety and protection because you don't have a clear understanding of privacy and strategies to keep yourself safe, especially when arguments arise or you have to agree to certain terms and conditions.

After all, understanding the digital world is complicated, so you might be discouraged by all the obstacles and dangers you might encounter online. However, like any other grandparent, you feel the urge to connect with your grandchildren and understand their world a bit more in-depth. You want to talk and stay close to them, so use this motivation to take the leap and discover the digital world. To master new technologies and improve your relationship with younger generations, convince yourself that you're not too old and you always have the power to improve—you just have to put in the effort and be patient. Don't listen to the inner voice that tells you that you don't have the right skills or to people who say that you'll never understand how to use digital tools.

Thanks to this book, you'll unlock the secrets of effective digital communication to bridge generational divides, build meaningful connections with your grandchildren, and master online etiquette. This book will be your all-in-one guide that will offer a fresh perspective and empower you to open your heart to technology, embrace new experiences, and have an open mind. In particular, Chapter 1 will provide basic, helpful information to navigate digital platforms confidently, and Chapter 2 will give you the tools to set up your accounts and create a profile successfully. Chapter 3 will be your "bridge" to understanding younger generations and how they use digital platforms.

Chapter 4 will dive deep into the importance of words in the digital realm and how to tell fascinating and engaging stories online. In Chapter 5, you'll learn to build strong and deep connections on the internet through empathy, compassion, and authenticity. In contrast, in Chapter 6, you'll discover how to handle conflict to ensure healthy and positive interactions. Chapter 7 will focus on netiquette (or digital etiquette) and how to stay safe online. Finally, Chapter 8 will provide valuable and practical tips to balance digital and face-to-face interactions to build stronger relationships with younger generations.

After writing *Beyond Emojis*, I felt the need to keep exploring the topic of digital communication from a new perspective—the one of nondigital natives. I wanted to ensure that not only younger generations but also older ones could feel safe and confident in navigating the digital landscape. My objective with this book is to bridge the communication gap between generations and help all grandparents create a deep connection with their grandchildren and younger ones. I want them to understand that effective communication is just as crucial in the digital world as it is offline, and they have the power to achieve it. Thanks to my experience in communication and background in both tech and education sectors, I aim to equip everyone to express themselves confidently and safely online, ensuring that communication skills aren't compromised in this fast-paced, technology-driven world.

And that's exactly what this book is about. Thanks to it, you'll not only understand the basics of digital platforms and communication, but you'll also uncover the secrets to online safety and effective and positive interactions with everyone. After reading, you'll be able to set up your accounts and use social media effectively. Moreover, you'll have the tools to engage in interesting and meaningful conversations about the digital realm with your grandchildren so that you can talk more with them, share your ideas and thoughts, and build a deeper connection.

# CHAPTER 1

# TECH TALK

## A WALK THROUGH TODAY'S DIGITAL LANDSCAPE

The world has changed a lot lately, hasn't it? I'm sure you still remember the time when people used their phones only when it was strictly necessary and preferred seeing each other face-to-face to develop deep connections. If they wanted to send a long message to someone, they couldn't send a three-minute audio on WhatsApp or make a video call—they had to use snail mail. Do you remember how you met your significant other or the things you used to do with your friends when you were younger? When your grandchildren tell you about their relationships and how they talk to their peers, you might feel confused and surprised by how things have drastically changed in so little time. But what happened in particular? In this chapter, you'll discover the main changes communication has undergone and how digital communication can improve your life. Then, you'll learn basic, useful information on how the internet works and what digital trends are.

## TALKING THROUGH THE YEARS

Let's take some steps back to understand how communication evolved. Since human beings have inhabited Earth, it has been paramount to interact with others and express our needs and wants. However, it hasn't always been easy: We started to communicate through speech around 102,000 years ago, but we weren't very good at it, so expressing our thoughts and emotions was complicated. That's why our first communication channel was cave painting—primitive but effective. As millennia passed and we developed new skills, we began to use petroglyphs and then pictograms to represent objects, concepts, events, activities, and places. Pictograms aren't so different from symbols we still use today, like road or nonsmoking signs (Mather, 2022).

Over 2,000 years ago, we invented a creative method to convey a message from one person to another: carrier pigeon. Thanks to our winged friends, we managed to "deliver" important information from one place to another, even different cities and countries. We can easily say that pigeons could be compared to an ancient postal system, which already existed in 2,400 BC in cultures like Egypt, India, Rome, Persia, and China. However, it only involved sending out decrees and similar things. In fact, the postal system as we know it today—the one you probably used more than once to send letters and postcards to your loved ones—was invented in the 17th century. This advancement was fundamental for the future development of communication, as it produced more changes in the last 2,500 years than all the thousands of years before (Munoz, 2017).

In the 15th century, the printing press system was developed, thus giving origins to newspapers. Three centuries later, the telegraph was invented, immediately followed by a new, revolutionary communication channel: radio. At the end of the 18th century, Alexander Graham Bell introduced the landline telephone, which allowed people from all over the world to communicate with loved ones from the comfort of their houses. In 1926, the television started entering people's houses and influencing their lifestyles. If you think about it, important technological advancements developed in just three or four centuries. It's easy to see all the progress we've made thus far, but that's just the beginning (Mather, 2022).

In fact, everything changed when the mobile phone was invented in 1984. In the beginning, people could only call one another, but that was already considered an incredible advancement because they could bring their mobile phones everywhere, from their offices to their cars and social gatherings. However, a new fundamental step forward was made in 1992 when SMS was introduced, and people could send messages to one another. In the meantime, computers began to be built and used by the public in 1991, and the internet, which was created in 1983, became an essential tool in all households. From that moment onward, everyone had access to the World Wide Web and could navigate online (Mather, 2022).

However, the real game changers came between 2004 and 2007 when Mark Zuckerberg invented Facebook. A few years later, Steve Jobs brought the World Wide Web to his first iPhone, giving everyone the opportunity to access the internet from their phones. Zuckerberg began a revolution that continues today, as he invented the first social media platform, which allows people to gather together and talk online. At the same time, Steve Jobs made the combination of mobile phones and the internet possible, thus inducing people to use social media on their phones and not computers (Munoz, 2007). From that historical moment a bit more than a decade ago, our lives have drastically changed, and social media has become the most fundamental communication channel. Without it, many people wouldn't know how to keep in touch with their friends and family. In little time, the internet has replaced all other forms of communication, making letters obsolete.

## THE POWER OF TECHNOLOGY AND WHY YOU SHOULD EMBRACE IT

Communication technology seems hard to understand and useless, as you can communicate with your loved ones with your landline or mobile phone, and you don't need to send texts on WhatsApp or use video calls. As you've lived in an era when these tools weren't necessary, you know how to live without them. But is this what you really want? Couldn't communication technology improve your life in some way? Digital literacy is paramount to understanding the basics of modern gadgets, smartphones, and computers, and many studies have found that it can significantly enhance the overall quality of life of older adults. This is true, especially for those who live alone or far away from their children and grandchildren and those with mobility constraints. Thanks to digital and communication technology, elders can be more independent, autonomous, and happier. However, studies show that more than 85% of them can be considered digitally illiterate, thus lacking the basic skills needed to understand the online world (Sharma, 2019).

Those who don't embrace the power of technology might face numerous challenges, like loneliness and isolation. If you don't know how smartphones and computers work, you might feel isolated from the rest of society, especially younger generations. Moreover, you might feel disconnected from your family, as your children and grandchildren communicate via Whatsapp and social media while you can't manage to keep pace with them. By learning the basics of digital technology, you empower yourself to reconnect with your loved ones and keep updated with what happens in their daily lives. Wouldn't you want to wish a good day to your grandchildren every now and then by sending them a simple message? I guess so, like many other grandparents would.

Digital technology also improves the overall quality of your life by making it easier and making you more autonomous. By now, you can't do anything without a smartphone and some essential apps, not even call for a taxi or Uber to go to the hospital, order groceries from the comfort of your house, or book an appointment with your doctor. If you know how to use smartphones and computers, you won't only stop being dependent on family, friends, and neighbors, but you'll also feel more self-confident and competent by completing tasks on your own. In addition, digital technology provides numerous opportunities to have fun and try different activities, like Netflix, online libraries, and much more. Last but not least, smartphones and computers can optimize your health and safety by giving you the opportunity to get remote consultations from your doctor, measure your health conditions with specific apps and tools, or install emergency alert devices.

How can you embrace the power of digital communication technology? Start with asking for help to practice using technological devices and have first-hand experiences with smartphones and computers. Therefore, involve someone in your journey to understanding and using digital technology. For example, you can ask for help from your children or grandchildren or another important person in your life who's good at using new technological devices and has time to show you how to do it. At the same time, start as simple as you can—look for smartphones, computers, and apps that are user-friendly, which means that they're very easy to use and intuitive. If you have visibility problems, I also suggest checking the settings on your devices to increase the size of the icons and text so that you don't struggle to read and look for information. It might seem like an insignificant tip, but it can actually enhance your overall experience and satisfaction with using technological tools.

Like any other activity or skill you want to learn, practice is essential, so make sure you dedicate enough time to using your smartphone and computer more than once a day. Whenever you can, try to do something with them—even just text "Hi" to your children. The more you practice, the more rapidly you'll learn how to use technological devices. An effective trick to learn faster involves connecting technology with your daily activities. For instance, set medication reminders, try to order groceries, or read the news online. The key to embracing digital technology is to be patient and take all the time you need. Keep in mind that you have to put effort and commitment into improving your skills and becoming good at using smartphones and computers, so do things at your own pace and don't rush the learning process. You shouldn't aim to learn as many skills as you can in as little time as possible but understand and use what's truly important to you and enhances the quality of your life.

In fact, when entering the world of the internet, you might be tempted to try different apps or various things that catch your interest. However, remember your goal and focus on what is truly useful for you and can improve your daily life. Don't fall into the trap of useless apps or silly games that don't help you physically or psychologically. Instead, concentrate on the things that have an impact. If you want, one of the easiest and most effective tools you can use is YouTube, which allows you to watch all sorts of videos. If you need help understanding how to use your smartphone or computer and discover what might be more useful for you, that's a good start.

## INTRO TO THE INTERNET

Let's get hands-on and dive deep into the world of the internet. First of all, what is it? The internet is a global network of computers that connects a gigantic number of devices all over the world. This global network is actually composed of different types of networks, like cable, fiber optic, and wireless. When you connect to the internet, you directly connect to one of these networks and get access to the World Wide Web, a collection of billions of images and pages. How does it work? Every device, even your smartphone, has a unique address called an IP address. When you want to access a website like Amazon, your device sends a request through your IP address to the server where Amazon is hosted and then allows you to open it. In fact, technological devices communicate with each other through protocols, which are rules that dictate how data is formatted and transmitted across networks.

Is it too much? Let's look at it in detail. So, the internet is a network of computers that allows you to share data with other devices and navigate online. When you search for information on the internet, you use web browsers, which are software programs that allow you to access, view, and navigate the World Wide Web. You can use Google Chrome, Mozilla Firefox, Apple Safari, or Microsoft Edge. Once you open Google Chrome, for example, you need to type what you want to look for on the internet. This operation is possible thanks to the search engine, the most popular of which is Google. When you find what you're looking for and click on the website you want to open, you get directed to its URL or Uniform Resource Locator, which is the address of a specific web page on the internet. The URL is easy to recognize because it always starts with "https:/," which represents the protocol or the rules that say how data is formatted and transmitted.

To navigate the World Wide Web safely and consciously, you need to know that there are four different types: Web 1.0, Web 2.0, Invisible Web, and Dark Web. Web 1.0 is composed of rudimentary graphics and plain text, so it's very simple. Web 2.0 allows you not only to see web pages but also to interact with them, like video gaming or online banking. Thanks to Web 2.0, you can do things on the internet in addition to simply reading articles and pages. We all use it in our daily lives when we open our Gmail or Facebook account to send emails and chat with family and friends. The Invisible Web is, as you might guess, invisible to those who aren't supposed to find it. It's also known as the deep or hidden web, and if you don't possess the necessary credentials to access it or aren't allowed on a specific web page, you can't see it. In the Invisible Web, you usually find password-protected information, like personal banking statements. Finally, the Dark Web is as dark as you imagine it, as it conceals users' identities to prevent authorities from tracking their activities. That's why it's usually used by those who traffic illicit goods, like drugs, but also those who want to protect themselves from oppressive governments. Luckily, you won't stumble upon the Dark Web by yourself because you can access it only through complex technology.

## *Websites*

Now that we've taken a closer look at the internet in general, it's time to understand what websites are and how they work. Do you remember that, in the previous section, I mentioned the words "server" and "hosted" in the example of Amazon? Such concepts might be confusing right now, but they'll soon be clearer as they're strictly connected with websites. A website is a collection of web pages where you can find all sorts of information. To make a website available and accessible all over the world, it needs to be stored or hosted on a server, which is one of the millions of computers that compose the global network of the internet. If the website isn't hosted on any server, then you (and anyone else in the world) can't access it.

On the internet, you can find an infinite amount of websites with different purposes. For example, blogs talk about specific subjects connected to personal interests and hobbies, like music or gardening. An e-commerce website allows you to buy everything you want online, from shoes to gifts for your grandchildren. News and magazines are also online, so you can keep updated with worldwide news without turning your TV on or reading your favorite newspaper, which is probably available on the internet if you search for it. Another category of websites known as social media platforms allows you to talk with everyone in the world and includes Facebook and Instagram. In addition to all of that, websites can offer educational content, become a sort of freelancer resume, or connect you with particular institutions like hospitals or schools.

Each website is different but shares a similar structure. In fact, all of them are characterized by the following components:

- **Web host:** It's the physical space where the website is stored. Without it, the website can't be accessed.
- **Domain:** Simply, it's the name of the website that allows you to find it online.
- **Homepage:** Each website is composed of one or more pages, of which the most important one is the homepage, the one you access first and that provides all the connections to the other pages.
- **Design:** It's all the visual part of the website and what people tend to judge. If a website's design is bad, it means that images, graphics, and visual effects inserted aren't appropriate and effective and people struggle to navigate rapidly and intuitively. If you think about it, the design is the main (if not the only) thing you notice in a website.
- **Content:** It's composed of all the information you find on a website, which can be written words but also videos or audio. The more engaging and

effective the content, the more people like the website.

You can find two types of websites: static and dynamic. Static websites have fixed content and appearance, which means that they look the same for all visitors around the world. Examples of static websites include portfolios and catalog sites that don't require much action on the visitor's part except clicking buttons. On the other hand, dynamic websites change content and appearance according to the visitors' location, what they search online, and what they tend to purchase. Examples of dynamic websites include Amazon and social media platforms, which allow you to interact in more complex ways, like paying to buy a product or sending a direct message.

## *Online Communication*

People use the internet for almost everything nowadays, but the most common use is undoubtedly to communicate with others. Online communication is any form of communication that happens on the internet and uses different types of channels. Social media includes Facebook, Instagram, Twitter, YouTube, LinkedIn, and many more platforms that allow you to keep in touch with people all over the world, share your ideas, or connect with companies and professionals around the globe. Instant messaging is a type of communication channel that is specifically designed to send texts, messages, videos, and audio. The most popular example is WhatsApp, but Facebook Messenger and Skype are also used worldwide. However, Skype doesn't only allow you to send messages, but you can also video call other people. In fact, it's both an instant messaging and video-calling communication channel. Apps that allow video calling became extremely common during the pandemic when people couldn't see each other in person, so they met online, and offices were closed, so workers stayed at home. Email is another communication channel that has been around for decades, but it's still prominent thanks to its simplicity and safety. In general, instant messaging apps are used to send informal texts to friends and family, while emails are more formal and mainly used by companies.

## DIGITAL TRENDS AND INNOVATION

After an overview of what happened in the past and how the internet has changed over the decades, it's time to focus on the present. As you've probably noticed by now, the digital landscape keeps changing and evolving rapidly. The moment you understand what Instagram is and how it works, TikTok suddenly appears, and you struggle to grasp it. This phenomenon involves not only social media platforms but also the internet and online communication in general. Every year, new trends arise, adjusting the way we interact with new technologies. The most popular and controversial advancement that has been made recently is Artificial Intelligence (AI), which is a technology that enables digital devices to learn, create, write, read, and analyze. In other words, AI allows machines to think like humans (almost).

A concrete example is Siri, the virtual assistant that is installed on all Apple devices and directly interacts with their owners. If one of your family members has an iPhone, you've probably heard them say at least once things like, "Hey Siri, call 'Mom,'" "Hey Siri, how's the weather?" or "Hey Siri, remind me to go to the post office tomorrow morning at 10." These are just examples of interactions people can have with Siri. It's considered an AI tool because it's capable of recognizing different voices and providing appropriate answers to people's queries, thus meaning that it's "intelligent."

AI tools have become more and more popular and keep evolving. Nowadays, they're used to develop new trends, like hyper-personalization, smart content, and chatbots. Hyper-personalization refers to a trend in personalizing content, products, and services based on customers' needs and wants. Until now, companies have created more engagement by using your first name, location, or previous buying habits to convince you to buy or use their products. Thanks to AI, they can now understand your lifestyle even better and create more complex experiences that are targeted to you specifically. Therefore, if you're used to using your smartphone between 2 and 4 p.m., you're more likely to see advertisements for products that interest you in that range of time.

Another trend consists of generating smart content thanks to tools like ChatGPT and Gemini, which might sound familiar due to the renowned debate surrounding them. To put it simply, you can ask them whatever question you want, and they'll provide a detailed answer. For instance, you can ask them how to open a business, plant flowers in your garden, or learn a new skill. They're not very accurate yet, and an expert eye can recognize AI-generated versus human-generated content, but they're powerful tools. When talking about content, I don't refer only to text but also to images, audio, and videos. Thanks to AI tools, you can create whatever image you have in mind or turn text into speech.

Finally, chatbots have been around for some time, replacing customer service. Until a few years ago, if you had a problem with a particular website or company, you had to call them or send them an email. Response time was very slow, and customer service had to work hard to assist everyone. When chatbots arrived, customers didn't have to call and communicate with real people anymore; they could simply direct their queries to AI tools that provided generated answers. As AI tools grow and become more complex, chatbots will be better at answering queries and helping customers around the world.

These are just some of the current trends that will define the future of digital communication. We started by uncovering the history of communication from the beginning of time and arrived at the latest innovations. We've already learned a lot, but we've just scratched the surface. In the next chapter, we'll dive deep into digital communication and take a closer look at the world of social media.

# CHAPTER 2

# CLICKING KEYS, OPENING DOORS

## UNLOCKING DIGITAL COMMUNICATION

S tatistics show that more than 60% of the world's population uses social media, and that percentage is likely to go up in the next few years. In the US, millennials— people between the ages of 27 and 42—are the ones who use social media more than any other. Gen Z—those between 11 and 26 years old—comes next, with more than 56 million. Then, almost 52 million people from Gen X—between 43 and 58—and only 36.9 million Boomers—those between the ages of 59 and 77—use social media. Statistics also show that, on average, people spend almost two and a half hours per day on such platforms, which means that this activity has become important in our daily lives. Although they have evolved and new ones have been created over the years, Facebook is still the number one social media platform used around the world, and its users are mainly adults (*The 2024 Social Media Demographics Guide*, 2024).

While the social media landscape may seem vast and complex, it's not beyond your grasp. By mastering the most popular platforms, you not only enhance your understanding of new technologies and trends but also foster stronger connections with those around you, particularly younger generations. This is why the following sections will delve into the world of social media, guiding you on how to set up your accounts, cultivate a positive online persona, manage your digital identity, create an effective profile, and navigate the most popular platforms with confidence.

## SETTING UP YOUR ACCOUNTS

The most popular social media platforms out there are Facebook, Twitter (which is now called X), Instagram, and TikTok. Therefore, we'll focus on them and uncover all the steps to set up an account in each one. LinkedIn is another well-known platform you've probably heard about, but it's mainly used to connect potential employees with companies and find a job online.

## *Facebook*

1. Open your web browser and search for "facebook.com."

2. Enter the website. At the right part of your screen, you'll see that you have the opportunity to "Sign up."

3. Fill in all the information needed, including your first and last name, email, and birthday. Pay particular attention when deciding on a password: Avoid using just one word or less than eight characters to ensure your online safety.

4. Click on the button "Sign up" in the bottom right corner.

5. A new page opens up where you have to complete three essential steps. The first one asks for more specific information about where you live and where you attended school or college. Fill it in, as it will be useful for creating your profile later on.

6. Step two consists of choosing your interests. You have to look at a list and select the things that are closer to your personality, like movies, music, and so on. If you want, you can skip this part by clicking on "Skip" in the bottom right corner.

7. Step three involves uploading a picture of yourself, which is not mandatory, so you can skip this step, too—you'll have plenty of time to upload a photo. Otherwise, click on "Upload a Photo" and select a

picture from the ones you saved on your computer or smartphone. When you've done it, you can click on "Save & Continue."

8. You finally open Facebook and see how it works! Before doing anything, please verify the email you've inserted when signing up to ensure that it's associated with you and not another person. Then, it's time to set a proper profile. You'll discover how to do it later in this chapter.

## *Twitter/X*

Once you manage to set up your first account, setting up the others becomes easier, as the steps are very similar. Now, let's look at "X," which was known as "Twitter" until a few years ago.

1. The social media has changed its name so recently that when you search for it, you can type "twitter.com."

2. Enter the website and click on "Get started."

3. Write down your name, the username you would like to use, a password, and your email address.

4. Type the words shown in the picture into the box you see on your screen. This is to make sure that you're a human being and not a computer program that is trying to create a fake account.

5. Click on "Create my account."

6. On the next page, you'll be asked to use your email account or other social media platforms to look for friends who already use Twitter. If you want, you

can add them in this stage or click on "Skip this step" and do it at another time.

7. Next, you see a list of the most popular users you might want to follow. By default, they're all selected, so if you don't want to add them to your Twitter account, un-check their boxes.

8. Click on "Finish" at the bottom of the page.

9. Your account is officially set, and you can use Twitter!

### *Instagram*

Instagram and Facebook are owned by the same big company, which is called Meta. Therefore, they're strictly connected, and creating a profile on one social media platform will facilitate the process on the other. If you've already created a Facebook account, here are the steps you must take to create your Instagram profile.

1. The main difference between Instagram and the social media platforms discussed above is that it's not a website but an app, so you must search for it on your Google Play Store or App Store.

2. Download it and open it on your smartphone.

3. Immediately, your Facebook account shows up, and you have two options: Connect the two social media apps or not. Click on "Continue as [your name]" if you want to connect your Facebook and Instagram accounts or "Create a new account" if you don't.

4. If you connect your accounts, you just need to click on "Yes continue" and then "Next" to synchronize all your information, like your profile picture and personal data. If you don't connect your account, click on "Continue without Facebook."

5. Create a username for your Instagram account and click on "Next."

6. Read Instagram terms and conditions and click on "I agree" to confirm that you have read and accepted them.

7. Now you're ready to use Instagram!

## *TikTok*

Like Instagram, TikTok is an app, so you have to download it from your Google Play Store or App Store. Let's look at the fundamental steps to create an account:

1. Open the TikTok app on your smartphone.

2. At the bottom of your screen, click on "Sign up."

3. On the next page, you'll be given the option to choose how you want to sign up for TikTok. If you want, you can use your Facebook or Twitter account, your email or phone number, or your Google or Apple account. As happens with Instagram, signing up with other accounts means that your contacts and personal information are automatically synchronized, so you don't have to do much.

4. If you decide to sign up with your phone number or email, click on this option and move to the next steps.

5. Enter the date of your birthday and click on "Next."

6. Decide if you want to open your account with your phone or email. Then, enter your phone number or email account and click on "Next."

7. Create a new password, remembering that it needs to be strong, and click on "Next."

8. Create a username and click on "Confirm."

9. Then, you'll be asked to answer some simple questions. You can synchronize your phone contacts. If you want to, click on "OK;" if you don't want to, click on "Don't allow."

10. You're also asked if you want to have personalized ads, which means that TikTok will show you ads based on your preferences and activities on the app. If you agree, click on "Accept;" otherwise, click on "Manage settings" and uncheck the box to personalize your ads.

11. Your TikTok account is ready!

If you need visual aids to set up your accounts properly, check YouTube to find plenty of videos on how to set up all the above accounts with step-by-step guides.

## THE IMPORTANCE OF HAVING A POSITIVE ONLINE PERSONA

Setting up social media accounts might not be that hard, but using them properly requires thoughtfulness. Nowadays, what you do and say online is as important as what you do and say in the real world, or even more. That's because you must always keep in mind that what you do online will stay there forever—there's no way to delete content or a comment once and for all. This means that everyone at this historical moment and the people who'll come next will be able to look at your online activity and understand who you were from what you did and said online. In addition, your online persona is strictly connected to your online and offline reputation: The things you do on the internet are very likely to have consequences in your real life.

Just think about the CEO of a big company who put pictures of his hunting trip in Africa. He upset so many people—especially his customers—so much that his company lost many clients, and his reputation fell significantly. This is valid not only for wealthy CEOs who are known around the world but also for every one of us. Families have been shocked and divided by Facebook or Instagram posts where members revealed their positions on hot topics, like immigration and politics in general, and appeared to be very different from what the other family members believed. For all these reasons, it's paramount that you pay attention to what you share online and build a positive online persona.

Like a negative online persona has adverse consequences on your offline and online world; a positive one has incredibly positive effects on your daily life. By sharing posts that bring joy, happiness, and curiosity, you support the development of a healthy world and deepen your connections with your family and friends. The main benefit of developing a positive online persona is that it represents all your qualities and skills. By being positive, you emphasize the things that you like and that make you a better person, not only online but also offline. The more you represent yourself positively on the internet, the more favorable your offline reputation will be. Therefore, avoid sharing posts and comments that spread hate or conflict online and focus on topics that unite people. By building a positive online persona, you show people that you feel free to express yourself without judging or hurting others. You value your opinion and respect others at the same time, so you spread positive vibes among your friends and followers. As you can see, underestimating the effects of your online persona in the online and offline worlds might lead to negative consequences for you and the people around you, so pay attention to what you share and do.

## UNDERSTANDING AND BUILDING YOUR ONLINE ID

Let's look more in detail at what "online identity" stands for and how to make it more positive. This concept is linked with your online persona and reputation and refers to the things you do and say online. If your offline identity refers to your activities in the real world and who you are in your daily life, your online identity revolves around everything you do on the internet. That's why, in the previous section, we talked about representation. The things you do and say in the real world represent who you are as a person, just like the things you do and say online.

Your online identity is not so different from your offline one. To build it, the first thing you must do is create a username, as you already discovered in this chapter. Your username corresponds to your online name and can be your first and last name. If your name is James Sullivan in real life, you can use "James Sullivan" as your username online. Alternatively, you can use an alias or a screen name that is different from the one you use in your daily life. This is particularly helpful if you want to protect your offline identity and don't feel comfortable sharing your real name online.

Another essential element of your online identity is your profile, which corresponds to basic information about who you are and what you like and includes a picture of yourself to show others how you appear in real life. Your profile reveals your authentic self and helps others understand what you enjoy, so it's important to set it up properly and share appropriate information. For instance, you can show others you're passionate about literature or cinema by sharing your favorite books or movies and talking about them.

Last but not least, status updates are an integral part of your online identity and involve everything you share online, from comments to thoughts and posts. They have a great influence on your reputation because they help others understand your point of view on different topics, so think twice before sharing any information. In addition, remember that what you share will stay there forever and can be seen by potentially anyone in the world, so avoid discussing personal issues that you don't want others to know about.

To develop a positive online identity, start with searching for information about yourself on the internet. You just need to access your web browser and type your name in the Google search bar. Then, look at all the results. You'll probably be surprised by all the things you find online about yourself, from friends and family who shared pictures of you to local news or institutions that shared your name online. If you find some information you don't feel comfortable sharing with the rest of the world, ask for help to get it immediately removed. After deleting the things about yourself you don't want to be associated with your online identity, it's time to build a positive persona!

## PUTTING THE "PRO" IN PROFILE

Now that you've set up your social media accounts and know what an online identity is, build up your profile and make it effective. The fundamental element of all profiles is your picture, obviously, because that's what people will first notice, and that will help them recognize who you are. That's why you must pay attention to the picture you use and choose a photo properly. Remember to always show your face so that others can easily identify you, and choose a picture that is not too close up or far away so that others can see your face but not your whole body. When you pose for a picture for your social media accounts, try to smile so you appear open and friendly. Finally, make your photo as personal as possible by introducing some details that help others understand who you are and what you like. Therefore, choose the right outfit and location to take the picture. If you enjoy spending time with your family while having lunch together, you can take a picture when you sit at a table surrounded by your loved ones (you don't have to show all your relatives, just make others understand that there are people around you).

After perfecting your profile, focus on the things you write, especially your social media bio, which is a few lines that describe who you are, what you like, and what you do. The more open and honest you are, the more your online persona will be positive, and people will feel like connecting with you. Pay attention to the words you use and focus on what you like doing. Then, choose your interests and friends carefully because they will define who you can connect with in the future and the posts you're more likely to stumble upon on your social media accounts. When setting them up the first time, you were asked to share your interests and start following other people or pages. If you didn't do it at that moment, you can do it right now. Think about the things you like and share your interests. For example, start following famous actors, authors, or politicians whom you admire and consider an inspiration. Next, follow pages that share your interests, like cooking, gardening, or watching specific TV shows. Make sure that your online persona is consistent throughout your social media accounts by following similar (or the same) pages and people on all platforms.

## NAVIGATING THE ONLINE JUNGLE

Let's explore how to navigate the online jungle and use the most popular social media platforms effectively. In fact, they all have different purposes.

- **Facebook:** Once you set up your account and profile, you can look for friends to add. Go to the search bar in the top left corner and enter the name of your friend or family member you want to add to your friends. Then, click on "Add friend" and wait for them to accept your request. If you add the wrong person, there's no problem, as you can easily unfriend someone. If you want to share something, you just click on the bar where you see "What's on your mind?" and start typing if you want to write, or upload a file from your computer or smartphone if you want to share a photo or video. After adding some friends, you can chat with them via Facebook Messenger. This social media is mainly used to connect with friends, loved ones, and people all over the world.
- **X/Twitter:** Twitter is all about sharing your opinion on current topics. In fact, the main thing users do is tell their followers what they think about a particular event or situation. When big occasions occur, like the night of the Oscars, Twitter users

find themselves online commenting on the awards and what actors do and say. The main difference between this social media and Facebook is that, in this case, you not only connect to friends and people you know but also with celebrities. The fundamental concepts linked with this social media are "hashtags," "tweets," and "retweets." Hashtags are keywords that are preceded by the pound symbol and are used to talk about specific topics, like the night of the Oscars. If you want to talk about that specific theme, you can use hashtags so that others can easily find what you wrote, leave a comment, or share your point of view. Tweets are comments you write, while retweets are comments that are left by other people on Twitter and that you share in your profile. When you retweet, it's usually because you agree with someone else or think their opinion is important and want to share it in your profile.

- **Instagram:** The focus of Instagram is sharing photos or videos, so you're always supposed to share that type of content on this platform. You can share or post single images, so you can share one picture and add a description if you want. On this social media, you can use hashtags like on Twitter, so if you post a photo of a family dinner, you can write down something like #familydinner. You can use as many hashtags as you want. Carousel posts allow you to share more images at the same time. For instance, if you go on a day trip with your loved one and take some pictures, you can share all of them at once, although you have a limit of 10 per post. Instagram reels are videos of up to 90 seconds that show everything you can think about, from a fast recipe to cats doing funny things. Instagram stories are images or videos that can be seen just for 24 hours. If you post a story at 2 p.m., your followers will be able to see it until 2 p.m. the next day. Finally, Instagram Live allows you to go live on video. The main form of interaction is through little hearts you find at the bottom left corner of every post. By clicking on them, you send a "like" to tell the author of that particular post that you liked what they shared.

- **TikTok:** TikTok is very easy to use because it only allows you to see and share videos, so you can't upload photos or simply share your opinion in written form. You only have two sections: *For You* and *Following*. The first one allows you to look at all the videos around the world based on your preferences and interests. If you like cooking, you're more likely to watch videos about people who cook and explain recipes. The second section shows only the videos shared by people you follow on TikTok. In this case, too, you find a little heart in the bottom left corner of each post that you can click on to show you like that video.

In this chapter, you learned the basics of social media platforms. You discovered how to set up your accounts, what an online identity is, and how to make it positive. You also learned some tips to perfect your profile and use social media effectively. At this point, the digital landscape might still appear a bit blurred and complicated, as you've only scratched the surface. In the next chapter, you'll find out more about how younger generations communicate online, how to understand their language, and how to use the same tools to interact on social media.

# CHAPTER 3

# INSIDE THE MIND OF A DIGITAL NATIVE

The form of content that fills our social media accounts more than others is emojis, which are images associated with specific ideas, feelings, symbols, or objects. Your children and grandchildren probably use them a lot while communicating with their friends and other family members, and you might have seen them already, as they're becoming more and more popular. But where do they come from? Their origins date back to the 1980s when people used "emoticons," which are pictures formed by punctuation marks combined. For example, people used ":-)" to convey a smile and happiness or ":-(" to represent sadness (Streets, 2023).

However, the father of emojis, as we know them today, was the Japanese artist Shigetaka Kurita, who invented the first ones at the end of the 1990s. In fact, the word "emoji" is a combination of two Japanese words that mean "letter" and "picture." That's exactly what an emoji is: a picture that represents a specific word. From that moment onward, emojis started spreading all over the world and being used in all messages and content shared on social media. Right now, younger generations use them to express their feelings and opinions (Streets, 2023).

Understanding the digital language that younger generations use to communicate can bridge the generation gap and foster better relationships. In the following sections, you'll discover that you have a lot in common with younger generations, and you have the power to understand the language they use. This includes learning how to use emojis and other fundamental digital tools, which can enhance your communication with them.

## NOT AS DIFFERENT AS YOU THINK

In the last decades, generations have been defined in different ways depending on their background and the period in which they were born. At the beginning of Chapter 2, we briefly introduced these definitions, but let's look at them in detail. Someone might have probably called you "boomer" at least once in your life—maybe even your grandchildren—and you might have wondered what it means. Boomers are also known as baby boomers and are the ones who were born right after the end of World War II, from 1946 to 1964 (more or less). This definition, like the others, is generic and doesn't delimit a specific period. Not everyone agrees that boomers are the ones born until 1964, but let's just take that date as a reference. Millennials are probably your children and include everyone who was born in the 1980s and 1990s. Finally, the words "Gen Z" are used to identify younger generations from the 2000s onward (*Similarities and Differences between Baby Boomers and Millennials*, 2022).

Apparently, these three generations have nothing in common because they were born in very different historical periods: Boomers saw the rise of computers when they were already old, millennials grew up with laptops and smartphones, and Gen Z has been completely surrounded by digital tools since they were born. This means that they all have different relationships with social media. But does this also mean that they're distant and can't understand each other? Not really, because they actually have many things in common.

Both baby boomers and millennials place great emphasis on family and community and use social media mainly to connect with their loved ones. They value close relationships and pay attention to their interactions. This similarity is probably because they've both grown up in contexts that united people and made them more socially conscious, especially concerning gender equality, religion, and sexual diversity. They both want to make a difference in their communities and want to create a better world for the generations to come. Moreover, they use social media to interact with like-minded people and share their interests, hobbies, and passions. If you think about it, what moves both generations is love for others.

Surprisingly, baby boomers share even more things with Gen Z members. First, they're both influenced by economic crises, as the former witnessed the Great Depression while the latter were impacted by the crisis of 2008. Therefore, they value financial goals and give importance to using money properly. Moreover, they both aim to bring about social change and do everything on their own, only using their resources and skills. Conversely, millennials are all about mentors and don't give importance to inducing big social changes. In addition, both baby boomers and Gen Zs are optimistic and resilient: They believe they can create a better world than the one they're living in and face obstacles with a positive attitude. This is probably due to the financial, economic, and global difficulties they've both encountered in their lives.

Although millennials also aim to provoke social change, Gen Zs are more similar to baby boomers because they're more politically active and spawn social movements all over the world. They're particularly interested in themes like climate change, abortion, gun control, and racism. But the similarities don't end there! Statistics show that both baby boomers and Gen Z enjoy traveling and love visiting new, distant countries all over the world. They share the same concern on climate change and are willing to change their lifestyles to do so: They would both cut out meat, eat more vegetables, switch to electric cars, and buy second-hand clothes.

Last but not least, both generations are willing to work harder for higher pay and aren't afraid of working long hours or during the weekend to increase their income (Brisinger, n.d.). All of this suggests that although Gen Zs were born with computers and smartphones, they're not so different from baby boomers. Consequently, although your grandchildren might appear distant or impossible to understand, they have more in common with your generation than you might think.

## SLANG

Communication occurs in many ways, but words are certainly the most used and powerful means. If you have ever looked at a chat between your grandchildren and one of their friends or heard them talking, you might have been confused by some terms, like "fam" or "ghosting." These are just two examples of the slang that younger generations use nowadays to communicate. To understand and interact with them effectively, you must enter their world and grasp the meaning behind their "weird" words. Here's a list of the most common terms younger generations use and their explanation.

- **Adulting:** When you were young, you probably didn't use this word because you were either a child or an adult, and there was no such thing as "adulting." However, important changes in our lifestyles and economic opportunities have made younger generations aware of the difficult moment between teenage years and finally being independent from their parents. As more young people go to college and complete training or internship programs, the stage between 18 and 30 years is becoming more and more important and is being defined as a period of "adulting," which corresponds to the transition between adolescence and adulthood.

- **Bae:** It's an acronym that stands for "Before Anyone Else." Younger people use it to identify their girlfriend, boyfriend, or their best friend.

- **CEO:** The term CEO is used in the business world to indicate the Chief Executive Officer, who is the highest-ranking person in a company. When younger generations use it, it's to define someone who is very good or a master at doing something. For example, one of your grandchildren might be the CEO of football if they're a very good football player.

- **Cheugy:** If something or someone is "cheugy," it means that they're not trendy or cool or they follow old-fashioned trends.

- **Clap back:** When you clap back, you criticize someone wittily. You can consider it a powerful comeback.

- **Fam:** The "fam" is the family, but not the one united by blood. If your grandchildren hang out with their fam, they're going out with friends whom they consider like family.

- **Ghosting/ghosted:** The term "ghosting" identifies the act of disappearing after having one or more dates with a potential partner. If your grandchild has been ghosted, they probably went out with someone they liked at least once and then texted for a while. From one day to the next, their flame simply disappeared and stopped answering their messages. The term "ghosting" refers to the fact that people who "ghost" disappear as if they were real ghosts.

- **Gucci:** You've probably heard of Gucci, the famous Italian brand of luxury fashion. Well, younger generations love it so much that they use that word to describe something that is good or that they love. If you hear someone say, "I'm Gucci!" or "This is so Gucci!" they mean that they feel good or love something.

- **Low-key and high-key:** When someone uses the word "low-key," it means that they're not 100% sure, while when they use "high-key," they're absolutely certain about something. Here are two examples of how you can use those words: "I'm high-key going out tonight" or "I'd prefer ordering a salad, but I'm low-key craving spaghetti." You can replace "high-key" with "certainly" or "for sure," while you can replace "low-key" with "kind of."

- **No cap:** This can be an intuitive term, as "cap" is an abbreviation of "capitalization." When you write something in cap, you want to emphasize it or even exaggerate your statement. If you use no cap, then you're not lying or using hyperbole to describe something. In other words, you're being honest.

You can use it in a sentence like this: "You're very clever, child. No cap."

- **Okay, boomer:** This slang is used to identify the differences between baby boomers and Gen Z. If your grandchildren answered "Okay, boomer" to something you said, you probably told them something that was linked with your generation and that has nothing to do with how younger generations are living now. To end the conversation rapidly and express frustration for the fact that you don't understand them, your grandchildren replied, "Okay, boomer." The conversation might have gone like this: They told you that they don't want to go to college right after finishing high school because they want to travel around the world for a while. You might have replied something like, "You can't travel the world; you need to go to college so that you can start working and earn a lot of money!" Then, they replied, "Okay, boomer," to close the conversation without arguing with you.

- **Shipping:** This term derives from "relationship" and refers to the desire to see two people being in a relationship. When you ship someone, you would like to see them together. For instance, you can say something like, "I ship these two actors because they would be perfect together."

- **Slay:** This word might seem too explicit and violent, but it means something completely different from what you might think. In fact, younger generations use it to emphasize when someone does something exceptionally well. If your grandchild says something like, "I slayed that test," it means that they passed it with high grades.

- **Squad:** It defines buddies or besties—in other words, loved ones. If your grandchild tells you that they're going out with their squad, you have nothing to worry about because they're just meeting their best friends. "Squad" and "fam" can be used interchangeably.
- **Stan:** It might look like a nickname for Stanley, but it's a combination of two words: stalker and fan. It usually defines a sort of obsession for a celebrity. The first person to use this term was Eminem in his famous song "Stan."
- **Sus:** It's just short for "suspicious."
- **TBH:** It's an acronym that stands for "to be honest," and younger generations use it as an abbreviation when texting each other.
- **Twerk:** It stands for a way of dancing that appears provocative and sexually suggestive. You've probably seen some celebrities twerk in their music videos or on social media.
- **Woke:** This term identifies a sort of awakening of younger generations in relation to political and social themes like racism or elections. If you're "woke," you're aware of what's going on politically and socially around the world and have a clear opinion about the latest news.

As you might have noticed, the above terms might appear obscure from the outside, but once you understand their true meaning and where they come from, you can grasp why and how people use them. Therefore, you're better able to understand your grandchildren when they talk with their peers or say something apparently incomprehensible to you. These are just some of the words younger generations use, but they help you get an idea of their slang. If you want, you can learn many more by talking to your grandchildren and being curious about the language they use.

## EMOJIS EXPLAINED

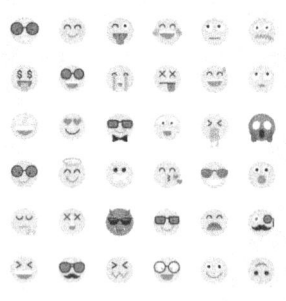

When talking with your grandchildren, you might notice some specific words you've never heard before. When you look at their texts, you might be even more confused by the symbols and images they associate with almost every word they type. As mentioned in the introduction to this chapter, such symbols are called "emojis" and are used to define emotions, objects, and much more. Although they might appear useless to you, they're a fundamental communication tool for younger generations. Thanks to them, they can convey clearer messages about what they think and want. When using texts, it's easy to misinterpret someone's words, especially if they're being sarcastic or joking. By adding an emoji at the end of a sentence, the sender can clarify what they mean and increase the chances that the reader will understand them. There are so many emojis that represent so many different things that you can use them to describe whatever emotion, action, and thought you can think about. They're very specific, thus allowing younger generations to express themselves clearly and avoid misunderstandings.

However, as you weren't born in this world, you might struggle to grasp the subtle differences between each emoji and how and when to use them. Below, you will find a list of the official names of the most popular ones to easily find on your smartphone or any application and social media platform and a brief explanation of what each one of them stands for.

| OFFICIAL NAME | MEANING |
| --- | --- |
| Grinning face | Cheerfulness and joy |
| Grinning face with smiling eyes | Happiness |
| Grinning squinting face emoji | It represents laughter after something hilarious has been said |
| Phew emoji | Relief |
| Tilted laughter | When something is hilarious |
| Face with tears of joy | When you laugh so hard that you shed tears |
| Heart face | Feelings of love and attraction |
| Blowing kiss | Goodbye to someone very close |
| Yum face | When you just had or are about to have a delicious meal |
| Crazy face | Kidding around, joking |
| Thinking face | Act of reflecting |
| Hugging face | Feeling of affection |
| Face with rolling eyes | When someone says something obvious or dumb |
| Sleeping face | Saying "good night" |
| Sleepy face | Feelings of tiredness and exhaustion |
| Smiling face with sunglasses | When you feel cool or something is considered cool |
| Fearful face | Feeling of fear |
| Loudly crying face | Inconsolable grief |
| Face screaming in fear | High degree of shock for unexpected news (can be both positive and negative) |

The most popular emojis are faces that express various positive and negative feelings, but they're not the only ones. If you open a chat with someone on WhatsApp, Instagram, Facebook, or any other social media, you'll find an endless list of emojis to choose from. In the beginning, there were only faces, but then they expanded and began to represent every thought, activity, event, and object. Nowadays, you can find emojis that represent different animals, fruits and vegetables, sports, transportation means, symbols, national flags, and much more. On the one hand, you have the power to communicate whatever message in a simple and clear way, but on the other hand; it might be confusing and overwhelming. If you feel like you'll never be able to understand the meanings behind all the emojis, there's nothing to worry about because nobody can. Even younger generations don't agree with the meaning of each emoji sometimes and inadvertently send mixed messages. To make sure you communicate effectively and don't get confused with all the emojis and their meanings, I suggest you use the most popular ones and nothing more. This way, you can remember them more easily and be sure that your message will be interpreted correctly.

## LAUGHING MATTERS

As you might have grasped from the above emojis, laughter is an important element in communication among younger adults. In general, laughter has incredibly positive effects on everyone's mental and physical health and is a good way of building and maintaining positive and strong connections with others. When we laugh, we release endorphins and relax our muscles, thus meaning that we feel calmer, and less stressed and anxious. Moreover, laughing improves our mood, self-esteem, productivity, creativity, and conflict-resolution skills. At the same time, it enhances our immune

system, cardiovascular health, and blood flow. By laughing, we see things from a renewed perspective and manage to connect with others on a deep level (*What Are Some Effective Ways to Use Humor?* 2023).

Have you ever been in a situation when something weird and unexpected happened, and you found yourself laughing with a stranger because you both assisted at the scene? Well, this is an example of how laughter can unite people, even when they don't know each other. If you think about it, millions of people go see stand-up comedy shows just to laugh and have fun. We can say that laughter is part of our human experience and allows us to improve the quality of our lives and relationships with others, so it's fundamental for our overall well-being.

The idea of laughing is always associated with humor, which involves joking and having fun with someone. However, there are different types of humor. The affiliate type is used to connect with other people positively and inclusively, thus telling funny anecdotes, jokes, or stories that don't hurt or offend anyone. Self-enhancing humor focuses on yourself and your ability to laugh at your mistakes and failures. This tool is particularly helpful when facing a challenge or hard time because it can lead you to see things from a different perspective and react positively to adversity. Finally, aggressive humor is about mocking or teasing others and can be dangerous because it might offend someone. For this reason, it's usually used among people who've known each other for a long time and understand when their loved ones have good intentions and don't want to criticize or judge them. In general, humor is a delicate topic because what someone finds funny might be considered offensive by someone else. That's why we must pay attention to the words we use and choose our jokes and stories wisely.

How can humor help you connect with younger generations? It's an integral part of their communication, so it allows you to deepen your connection with them. Let's start with millennials. They're famous for their dark, strange humor that is displayed in popular TV comedies like *BoJack Horseman* and *Rick and Morty*. They're cartoons that depict a reality completely different from the one we know and live in. Usually, something weird and unreal happens while the characters try to find their way out of everyday troubles. This type of humor can be considered self-enhancing because it allows millennials to look at their lives from a different perspective. As they have witnessed the world changing in front of them rapidly due to technological advancements and economic crises, they see it as daunting and unpredictable. That's why their humor is a bit dark and self-centered: They acknowledge they live in tough times and think that they lack the power needed to improve their situation (Aroesti, 2019). If you want, you can take a look at the cartoons mentioned to understand how millennials see themselves and the world around them.

While millennials focus on self-enhancing humor, Gen Z prefers absurdism or antihumor, which involves having fun by saying or doing absurd things that usually make no sense. For example, a famous TikToker once asked her followers if they wanted to help her create the plot of a fictional horror movie titled *Zepotha*. What her followers had to do was imagine how the horror movie could have developed and its main characters and then comment on other people's posts by saying that they looked exactly like *Zepotha*'s characters. As a baby boomer, you might not understand this form of humor and believe that it doesn't make sense. Well, most millennials would agree with you, as they also struggle to get a hold of Gen Z's jokes. At the same time, Gen Z's humor keeps evolving according to new trends, so it's hard to keep up with all the changes and understand why your grandchildren find something funny. To make sure you grasp their sense of humor, just be curious and ask them questions.

The world of humor is complicated and ever-changing, but you have the power to understand younger generations on a deeper level by putting yourself in their shoes and trying to grasp what they consider funny. In general, communication has completely changed in the last decades and is now based on slang, emojis, and apparently senseless jokes. In this chapter, you took the first steps toward the younger generations' world and understanding how they communicate. In the next one, you'll focus on words and how to use them effectively to build stronger and deeper connections.

# CHAPTER 4

# MASTERING THE ART OF WORDSMITHING

> *The purpose of a storyteller is not to tell you how to think, but to give you questions to think upon.*

— BRANDON SANDERSON

Words convey powerful messages, and that's why we must choose them carefully. At the same time, attention spans are getting shorter and shorter, so it's harder to keep people focused and convey our messages. In this chapter, you'll learn everything about attention spans, why they're getting shorter, and how to spark interest using just a few essential words. Then, you'll discover useful tips to craft meaningful emails and messages using the right tools.

## UNDERSTANDING ATTENTION SPAN

We all know what attention means: It's our brain's ability to focus on a particular object or thought without considering everything else inside or outside of us. When we pay attention to something, our brain concentrates on it and forgets about the place where we are, other objects around us, and other thoughts that might divert our attention. However, attention is a bit more complicated than that: The task we must accomplish, the environment, and our mental and physical health play a fundamental role in our attention. For example, we might maintain our attention for a longer time when we play silly games online, while we might struggle to focus while reading a scientific article. We're more engaged and concentrated after a good night's sleep than when we drink a lot of coffee or abuse other substances that might alter the quality of our sleep. Moreover, distractions around us impact our attention: If we're surrounded by people talking and things happening, we're less likely to maintain our focus for a long time. Conversely, if we perform the same task at home alone, we increase the chances of staying concentrated.

In general, human attention spans range between 2 seconds and 20 minutes, but nowadays, the average is 8.25 seconds. To give you an idea of how much it is, consider that the goldfish has an attention span of about 9 seconds, thus meaning that it manages to maintain its attention longer than us. How is that possible? Statistics show that the average attention span has kept decreasing in the last decades. In particular, it reduced by 25% from 2000 to 2015, which means that we're slowly losing our ability to stay focused for a prolonged time. Statistics show other surprising and alarming results. For example, 25% of teenagers tend to forget important details of their friends' and relatives' lives. Moreover, people get easily distracted: An office worker checks their emails around 30 times per day, and, on average, we pick up our phones 1,500 times per week, taking up more than 3 hours per day (Hollander, 2023).

The main reasons why our attention spans are reducing are social media and the internet. They're the best distractions for all of us because they allow us to take a break from the task we must accomplish without maintaining high levels of concentration. Our brains crave excitement, social connections, and novelty, which can be easily received from picking up our smartphones and scrolling social media. Due to these technological devices, our attention spans have changed and adapted to multitasking or moving from one task to another rapidly. In fact, they push us to look at numerous posts, pictures, and videos rapidly while scrolling and answering messages or comments. Every time we pick up our smartphones to take a break from another task, we force our brains to focus on a different thing. Then, we keep forcing them by practicing different activities while navigating social media and the internet. The more we switch tasks, the more our brains get used to wandering and looking for other ways to experience excitement, novelty, and social interactions. That's why many people say that social media is addictive:

The more you use it, the more you want to keep doing it, and this addictive nature should be a cause for concern (Ducharme, 2023).

## *Capturing Ever-Shortening Attention Spans*

When communicating with others, you must consider the average attention span, especially if you interact with younger generations. How can you capture their attention in a few words? Before saying anything, use a hook or headline to spark interest and convince them to keep reading your messages and posts. A hook is one or a few sentences that catch readers' attention, like the first words you hear in a TV commercial that wants to sell you a specific product. Let's say you want to discuss what your best friend did last weekend with your grandchildren. Avoid sending a text that starts with something like, "Yesterday, I was buying groceries at the supermarket, and I met my best friend. We talked a lot, and then they said something interesting." Instead, start your message with, "You can't imagine what my best friend told me yesterday!" This way, you not only include all the relevant information—and nothing else—but you also spark your grandchildren's interest.

To interact with younger generations effectively, you should also send short messages: Don't write 1,000 words to explain your opinion or discuss a specific point, but be straightforward and analyze the heart of the matter. In addition, use words and images or pictures at the same time. Therefore, accompany your messages with some catchy emojis, as you learned in the previous chapter, or send photos to show what you're doing before explaining it. For example, if you want to tell your grandchildren what your dog or cat did today, send a picture or video before saying anything so that they have an idea of what's going on. If the discussion risks being long and complicated, I suggest you call or send them an audio recording instead of writing a long message.

The way you use words has an incredible effect on the readers' concentration and might impact their attention span. One of the most useful tricks to maintain their interest is to use an active voice instead of a passive one. Instinctively, we all prefer an active voice because it's easier to read and understand, while a passive one requires more effort and concentration on our part. When talking to younger generations, pay attention to the voice you use and change all your verbs from passive to active. For instance, instead of saying, "My dog was saved by a kind and polite guy in the street," you can say, "A kind and polite guy saved my dog."

If you want to craft meaningful content for younger generations, you must also consider the value and relevance of the information you want to share. Sometimes, the reason why we don't manage to connect to younger ones is that we focus on events and thoughts that spark no interest in them. Your grandchildren might be curious to know what happens to your pet and if you maintain good mental and physical health, but they might not be interested in every detail of your friends' lives. I know you want to share everything with your grandchildren to create a strong connection with them, but quality is always more important than quantity, so choose the information you want to share carefully.

## *Tricks to Spark Interest*

When interacting with younger generations, you have the power to spark their interest in many different ways. By knowing the things they consider engaging and fun, you can take advantage of them to enhance your communication skills and convey more effective messages. One of the most popular trends that allows you to build a strong relationship is gamification. This word is used to identify all the things you can do and say to make readers have fun and feel like they are in a game. To gamify your messages, propose challenges or rewards if they understand what you're going to talk about next or guess your thoughts and emotions. Don't simply express what you have in mind, but involve them by asking them what they think about what you're saying or what they would have done in your place. Alternatively, propose different scenarios and ask them to choose the one they prefer or develop them as they please.

Another communication tool that you can use to interact with younger generations is storytelling, which has become popular in the last few years. Storytelling is the act of telling stories that grasp listeners' attention and make them feel engaged in the situation. Companies use storytelling to increase their sales by telling stories that consumers find interesting and captivating. Obviously, you don't have to become a professional storyteller or sell products like companies do, but you can use this tool to your advantage. When you tell a story to your grandchildren, for example, talk about different people involved and how they interact with you. Create characters by emphasizing some qualities and flaws that make them more interesting.

Moreover, make sure that you follow a clear structure so that your grandchildren know who the main character is, what problems they must face, how they achieve their goals, and what happens next. At the same time, make them reflect on the events by asking them questions about the characters or what might occur in general. People feel more engaged with stories when problems or conflicts arise, so try to emphasize these aspects and help your grandchildren understand how much the main character struggled to achieve the end result.

As you learned in the previous chapter, fun is an important element in younger generations' digital communication. To spark their interest, try to make the story funny or add humorous facts. If they don't know what to expect next or are caught by surprise, they're more likely to stay engaged and listen to you carefully. Therefore, try to insert shocking events, just like directors do in movies. Pauses and sounds are also effective tools to spark interest in your grandchildren and younger ones. If you talk to them, pause before revealing how you solve a problem or achieve a goal or introduce sounds to mimic weird objects involved in your story. If you send them a message, use ellipsis or send more texts to divide your story based on the main events and surprises.

When crafting stories for your grandchildren, keep in mind that you mustn't create things that happen to you but take inspiration from your real life and make simple events more engaging and interesting. In fact, younger generations value authenticity and genuineness.

## CRAFTING MEANINGFUL EMAILS AND TEXTS

The context in which you use words plays a crucial role in conveying the right message: Sending an email or a text is not the same thing. Although there are some rules that you can apply in both cases, you must also follow specific tips. Before writing an email or text, think about your goal: Why are you sending it? What do you want to say to the reader? What message do you want them to get? When you define your purpose, understanding which tone of voice and language to use becomes easier. If you want to text your grandchildren to ask about their day, you can write something like, "Hey, how are you?". In contrast, if you send an email to ask for detailed information about booking a room in a hotel, you might use a more formal tone and write something like, "Good morning, I have some questions about booking a room at your hotel. Can you clarify my doubts?"

After becoming aware of the purpose of your text and email, it's time to craft it. Remember that you usually start with a greeting, explain your situation, state what you need from the reader (if necessary), and apologize if you made a mistake or thank them in advance if you asked them to do something for you. Then, you close the text or email by wishing them a good day or something similar. The main difference between an email and a text is that the former is more structured and formal. Therefore, you must make sure you always greet the receiver of your email and provide detailed information. As texts are more rapid and entail quick responses, you don't need to greet your receiver all the time or close the conversation in some way. You can just start a new chat with "hey" and say what you want.

Before sending the message or email, remember to check grammar and punctuation more than once and eliminate all the mistakes. If you make an error when talking to someone face-to-face, you have the time and means to adjust your words and clarify your message. Conversely, written words are more likely to cause misunderstandings and misinterpretations because you don't directly talk to the receiver, and they have to interpret your words without any additional help from you—they just read what you say to them without looking at your body language and other important verbal and physical cues. For these reasons, clarity is paramount, and in order to achieve this, you must use correct grammar and punctuation. In addition, check your spelling and tone of voice. Reading your email or text out loud can help you understand if you're using the right tone or need to adjust it. Sometimes, you might feel like you're being polite and respectful when you might actually choose a more aggressive tone of voice. This is normal and happens to all of us—you just need to practice and pay more attention to the words you use.

When sending an email, an essential element you must check is the subject line, where you can write down a summary or brief explanation of the content of your email. If you use a bad subject line, you risk confusing the receiver and making them struggle to interpret your message. That's why you must make it short and direct. Let's imagine that you need to send an email to the hotel where you booked a room, as mentioned in a previous example. A bad subject line might look something like this: "Info about reservation for May 25th." This information isn't enough to help the receiver understand what you need from them and what you're referring to. The more specific you are, the more easily they'll interpret your words, so your subject line should be something like "Request for booking details, reservation number [...] from May 25th to June 2nd."

### Tips to Convey Your Message Effectively

Let's look at more detailed tips on how to craft meaningful texts and emails. When sending a text, make sure to keep the receiver in mind and use appropriate language to convey your message. Think about their preferences, needs, and interests to create a text that resonates with them. For instance, I'm sure you won't send the same message to your children and neighbors. In the first case, you might write something like, "Hey, can you accompany me to the post office tomorrow morning?" Conversely, in the second case, you might use more polite language and write something like, "Good morning! I need to go to the post office but, unfortunately, I can't go by myself. Would you be free and available to accompany me tomorrow morning? I would really appreciate your help." In addition, remember that messages are meant to be short, simple, and concise, so try to use as few words as possible. You can practice with SMS, which has a limited amount of words. By writing an SMS, you manage to keep track of how much you write and change your message accordingly. If the words are too many for an SMS, they're probably too many for any other messaging app, so reduce them. The clearer and more honest you are in your texts, the more easily you build trust, thus deepening your connection with the receiver.

Crafting meaningful emails might be simpler because you have much more space and can write more, but it doesn't mean that you don't have to pay attention to your language and tone. In general, emails are more professional than text messages, so you must be as clear as you can and use a positive tone of voice. One of the most common mistakes people make when sending emails is oversharing, which means that they share more information than required. Before sending anything, reread what you've written and ask yourself, *Is all of this necessary?* No matter who the receiver is, you might be tempted to go too much into detail, as happens to all of us.

Instead of adding a lot of information, encourage the receiver to ask you questions in case you've been unclear or omitted some essential information. The basic elements every email should include are the following:

- who you are
- what you want from the receiver
- why you want it, and why you're asking them
- why they should help you
- what the next steps are

As emails are longer than messages, the way you organize the text plays a crucial role in helping the receiver understand what you want from them. For this reason, it's always best to break it up and divide it into short paragraphs. Whenever you can, it may be helpful to use bullet lists so that the receiver can easily visualize the most important information. Keep in mind that paragraphs can also contain just two short sentences, so don't hesitate to break up the content of your email. Moreover, before sending it, make sure that you've inserted everything you need. One thing we all forget to check is attachments: We send emails saying that the receiver will find files attached but then forget to attach them, so we have to send a second email just for them. To avoid such situations, remember to check your attachments twice.

Sometimes, you might need to discuss different topics and don't know how to include everything in one email. If you realize that your message is too long and doubt that the receiver will be able to understand it, discuss a different topic in each email. Let's say you want to know the prices of a travel agency and ask them for more details about the place you would like to visit. Instead of including both topics in one email, start by asking the prices and see how they reply. When the conversation is closed, you can send another email asking them for more information about the place you want to visit. This way, you can both easily keep track of your conversation and stay on topic in each email. Last but not least, remember that emails are different from texts, so you should avoid using the same expedients to convey your message effectively. Although emojis and punctuation marks allow you to clarify your intentions in a text, they might sound inappropriate and unprofessional in emails, so don't include them.

In this chapter, you uncovered the significance of words and how they can impact the people around you. You discovered that the average human attention span is extremely limited, so you must make your content short, concise, and accurate. Then, you also learned some useful tips to craft emails and texts. In the above sections, we started talking about tone and context and how understanding the people you talk to is essential to crafting compelling stories. In the next chapter, we'll dive deep into the topic of empathy and ways to improve your digital communication skills.

# BRIDGING THE GAP ON A LARGER SCALE

*If you just communicate, you can get by. But if you communicate skillfully, you can work miracles.*

— JIM ROHN

There are plenty of books designed to help the older generation navigate the digital world more effectively, but this book isn't really about that. What we're dealing with here is more about communication than technology, and my goal is to help bridge the communication gap between older and younger generations. Effective communication is every bit as important in digital spaces as it is in spoken or written word, and the problem is that the digital landscape has evolved so rapidly that it hasn't been easy for older generations to keep up.

I think more people are realizing now that digital communication is just as powerful and complex as other forms, and they're beginning to worry that they've been left behind... So now that you're getting a better handle on it, I'd like to ask you to join me on my mission to help more people with that. The good news is, this requires very little work from you— I've already done it! All we need to do now is get this book into the hands of more of the people who are looking for guidance in this area... and all that requires is to make it more visible to them when they search for resources. The way this is done is through reviews: Reviews make it easier for people to find the information they're looking for and assess whether it's going to help them with what they need.

**By leaving a review of this book on Amazon, you'll help new readers find the guidance they're looking for quickly and easily—thereby helping to bridge the communication gap on a larger scale.**

We all live in the digital world, whether we're comfortable with it or not, and if we want to communicate effectively across the generations, this knowledge is vital.

Thank you so much for your support. You're making more of a difference than you realize.

### Scan the QR code below

# CHAPTER 5

# ON THE SAME WAVELENGTH

## CULTIVATING EMPATHY IN DIGITAL INTERACTIONS

> *When you talk, you are only repeating what you already know. But if you listen, you may learn something new.*
>
> — DALAI LAMA

Digital communication is different from real-life interactions in many ways, but the fundamental factors that help others understand and interpret your messages correctly are the same. In the following sections, you'll understand the significance of empathy and active listening skills in digital interactions and how to put them into practice to connect with younger generations. You'll also uncover generational differences in communication styles and how to amplify your messages based on them.

## ALL ABOUT EMPATHY

Empathy is a skill we should all possess and practice in our everyday lives, both online and offline. It's the ability to put ourselves in other people's shoes and take their perspective, thus understanding the feelings, thoughts, and reasons behind their behaviors. If your grandchildren tell you that they prefer playing video games at home during the weekend to going out with their friends, you might feel confused and struggle to understand how they could prefer staying in front of a screen instead of meeting their peers in person.

If you lack empathy, you might encourage them to get out of their room and have fun outside, thus forcing them to do something that you probably enjoyed at their age and that you find more important. Conversely, if you're empathetic, you acknowledge that the world has changed, and kids prefer doing different things from what you were used to. Therefore, you accept their decision and let them play video games. By becoming more empathetic, you learn to recognize and accept others' emotions and needs and feel how they feel. Consequently, you develop stronger and deeper connections with them as you make them feel understood and appreciated for who they are.

Being empathetic toward people who are similar to you is not difficult, as you easily put yourself in their shoes. However, you might find it hard to understand younger generations and technological advancements like social media. This is normal because you perceive them as distant from you and the world you're used to living in, but this doesn't mean that you can't become more empathetic or understand social media. The most effective way of building your empathetic skills is to connect with others, especially those who appear more distant from you. For instance, dedicate more time to talking to your grandchildren and understanding how they live. Let them show you how they use social media to interact with their friends and try to see things from their perspective.

Then, experience the world firsthand by using the same social media and putting effort into understanding it. Keep in mind that human connection is possible online. Like many others, you might believe that the internet is a malicious world where people don't talk to each other or create deep relationships, but just exchange likes and emojis. However, social media can be much more than that. In fact, not only can you leave a comment on the latest post shared by your grandchildren, but you can also send them a message to let them know how much you like what they've shared. Take advantage of the potential of the internet to build stronger relationships with your loved ones!

## RECOGNIZING THE SUBTLETIES OF TONE AND CONTEXT IN TEXT MESSAGES

When you interact with someone online, being empathetic might appear a bit harder than in real life for various reasons, the most important one being that you can't be sure about the message they want to send. When you talk to someone in person, you can look at fundamental cues that allow you to understand their true emotional state and what they want from you. For example, you can pay attention to their body language to interpret their words. Depending on their posture, position, and gestures, they might express positive or negative emotions. Moreover, their facial expressions and tone of voice allow you to immediately grasp if they feel happy, sad, or upset. If they don't make eye contact with you, they might feel ashamed or struggle to say something to you, while if they laugh and their tone of voice is a bit higher than usual, they probably feel excited. All these elements are lacking in an online conversation, thus increasing the chances of misinterpreting or misunderstanding their message.

Punctuation marks and emojis certainly help you understand how the person you're talking to feels. If they send an emoji with a smile or use exclamation marks, they're probably happy. However, these elements might not be enough to provide a correct interpretation of their message, and studies confirm it. In 2005, researchers divided participants into two groups: senders who had to send an email with ten different statements and receivers who had to interpret them. Unfortunately, receivers were able to identify if the senders were serious or sarcastic only 56% of the time, thus meaning they had a great chance of misunderstanding the message. To investigate the difference between written and oral messages, researchers tried the same experiment, but this time, senders had to send voice recordings. In this case, receivers correctly interpreted their words 73% of the time (Jaffe, 2014). These results show how sending a voice recording instead of a text can be enough to increase your chances of understanding what others want to tell you.

Why do we struggle so much to interpret written messages? The reason resides in our brains. When we lack information, we're hard-wired to use stereotypes, which are often negative, to fill the gaps. When receiving a message from someone, we tend to assume that they have bad intentions, so we reply accordingly, showing less empathy. What we forget is that most of the time, people have good intentions and don't want to hurt us. If you remember this, you'll respond with more empathy and improve your digital communication skills.

To increase your chances of correctly interpreting others' messages, focus on the words they use, as each one of them has a positive or negative meaning. For example, "cute" always refers to something positive, while "hard" usually has a negative connotation. Read the words carefully, and even if the message you receive seems confusing, try to understand if the sender uses more negative or positive words. Finally, pay attention not only to the quality but also the quantity of words used. If the sender uses very short sentences and simply replies with a "Yes" or "No," it might mean that they don't feel like engaging with you at that moment or don't feel like talking in general. Therefore, don't insist on sending more texts and asking more questions; just end the conversation. By doing this, you show empathy because you make others understand that you accept their feelings and won't force them to talk even when they don't feel like it.

## BRIDGING THE GENERATION GAP

As mentioned previously, understanding things that are close to you is easier than understanding something that is distant from what you're used to experiencing. The generation gap represents the differences between different generations and the reasons why you might struggle to put yourself in younger people's shoes. By becoming aware of this gap and learning more about younger generations, you have the power to reduce the divide and understand what they want and need. The generation gap is evident in our everyday lives and reminds us of the differences between children, parents, and grandparents. As a parent, you've probably noticed how different your kids were from you while growing up—and your grandchildren are even more!

But where does this generation gap come from? The most important factor is a change in opinions. What was considered unacceptable or outrageous in the past might be normal right now. Just think about how the fashion industry and dating have changed in the last century. In addition, we all fall behind at some point and are resistant to change. As we grow up, we feel connected to the things that characterized our childhood and adolescence and stick to them because we value them more than what younger generations consider cool now. After all, who has ever said, "Things were better before?" As we focus on what we liked when we were younger, we automatically miss some fundamental changes and don't manage to keep up with the latest advancements. At the same time, we struggle to adapt to new situations and technologies because we don't understand or value them as much as we do with our past.

How can you reduce the generation gap? Start with respecting everyone and accepting that each generation has different needs and wants. When you were young, you might have just wanted to work for the same company for your whole life because that was what everybody wanted. Right now, your grandchildren might be looking for various opportunities at different companies. Just acknowledge that they're different because they live in a new era. Moreover, practice empathy to see things from their point of view. Ask them questions about what they want and need, and be curious. As always, the most effective way of understanding others is to communicate with them, so take the time to have deep conversations with your grandchildren and other people and learn as much as you can about social media and the internet. Keep an open mind and be ready to accept a different reality from what you're used to or expect.

## Recognizing Generational Differences in Communication Styles

Now that you have an idea of what the generation gap is and why it exists, it's time to look at it in detail to truly understand younger people. The main difference between millennials and older generations is that they value their time and work-life balance. They see themselves not just as workers but as human beings who need to grow more than just on a professional level. Therefore, they give importance to the time they spend outside of work, taking care of their loved ones and practicing different hobbies.

Millennials also enjoy flexibility, so they prefer having the ability to choose where and how to work. For instance, they tend to value flexible working options more than just staying in the office and don't aim to work for the same company for their whole life. When they communicate, they prefer texts over any other form of communication and feel uncomfortable talking on the phone. When they call someone, they feel like they don't have enough time to think about what to say before saying it and interrupt people in the middle of their day. For these reasons, they think that messages are more precise and allow them to contact others without disturbing them. If your children are millennials, you probably recognize some of their traits in the above description.

As for Gen Z, they're completely different. They are more into instant communication and multitasking, so they expect things to move fast and can handle different tasks simultaneously. If your grandchildren are Gen Z members, you've probably seen them eating while answering a text from their best friend and watching a YouTube video. The only thing that Gen Z and millennials have in common is their love of texts, but for two distinct reasons. In fact, the former like sending messages because that's the fastest way to reach someone. Moreover, they're not used to engaging with long written content because they have a limited attention span, as you discovered in the previous chapter. If you send them a long text, they probably won't read all of it and will lose their attention easily.

Finally, as Gen Zs were born in a digital world where in-person communication is less and less common, they value face-to-face interactions and place importance on knowing and talking to someone in real life. When they interact with others, they look for equality and inclusion, feedback, and transparency. As they're one of the most socially active generations of the last century, they pay attention to the injustices that occur around the world and defend everyone's right to be respected and accepted as human beings—no matter who they are or where they come from. Moreover, they're used to receiving feedback and appreciate when someone shares their opinions, as they see it all the time on social media through likes and comments. Last but not least, they're aware of the importance of transparency due to the fact that they're growing up in a digital world filled with fake news and inaccurate data.

## *Understanding the Perspective of Younger Generations*

So, developing empathy and bridging the generation gap is all about perspective-taking, which is the ability to consider and understand others' thoughts, feelings, and experiences. When you take someone else's perspective, it's like you put aside your glasses and wear theirs so that you see the world from their eyes. If you develop perspective-taking skills, you reduce conflicts, especially with people who appear different from you, and enhance your conversations. You also become more self-aware because you acknowledge the differences between your and others' opinions and value both equally. At the same time, you grow as an individual because you're willing to learn from other people and understand how they live their lives. In addition, you strengthen your relationships and social connections because others feel comfortable talking with you and sharing their thoughts and emotions.

Practicing perspective-taking skills is essential because we're not as good as we think at interpreting others' thoughts and emotions, as research shows. When we listen to someone, we think we know what they have in mind and mean, but in reality, we analyze the situation from our personal point of view. Research has also found that real-life conversations are better than any other form of communication because we can pay attention to verbal and nonverbal cues that aren't present in online interactions (Shea, 2018). Having face-to-face conversations helps us all avoid misunderstandings and misinterpretations.

However, we can't always have face-to-face conversations, so we must find a way to communicate effectively through texts and social media. Even if you don't consider yourself to be a judgmental person, you probably see things from your perspective, like anyone else, so you must improve your perspective-taking skills. How can you do it? Simply stop assuming and start asking, even when you think you know exactly what's in someone else's mind. Among all the questions you might ask others to understand their point of view, the ones below are the most effective:

- **How do you feel?** Don't take emotions for granted, but always ask others how they feel after something relevant happens in their lives.
- **Did you expect this situation to go like that?** Keep in mind that different people interpret the same event differently, so avoid taking their point of view for granted.
- **Why do you say that?** Instead of assuming that you know the reasons behind someone's words, ask them why so that you are 100% sure about what they mean.
- **What do you wish people asked you about?** Sometimes, your questions appear useless, and you may feel like you can't empathize and

connect with someone. In such cases, the best thing to do is understand what they want and expect from others.

- **How can I help?** Don't assume that you know the answers to their problems and have the perfect solution, but ask them how you could help them so that you become aware of their true needs and wants.

## PRACTICING ACTIVE LISTENING IN ONLINE INTERACTIONS

Empathy is a fundamental skill strictly connected to active listening. If you don't listen, you're less likely to be empathetic toward others. When you communicate, you might believe you listen to what people tell you when, in reality, you think about something else. This is normal, as all human beings struggle to focus on someone when they talk, and their brains tend to multitask, so they think about other things that might not even be related to the conversation. However, listening to others is paramount to understanding their point of view and responding appropriately to their needs and wants. That's why you should develop active listening, which is the ability to be fully present in the moment and truly listen to people instead of just hearing. Practicing this skill allows you to create a deep bond with them and understand them on a deeper level like many others can't. Consequently, it helps you bridge the generation gap and put yourself in the younger generations' shoes.

When thinking about active listening, you probably imagine face-to-face conversations. In fact, listening involves using your ears, which is not required in online conversations unless you send voice recordings. However, active listening skills can be easily applied to the digital landscape to improve your interactions and communicate more effectively. For example, you can repeat or summarize the messages you receive from others. Let's imagine that one of your grandchildren tells you that they got a low grade at school, and they feel upset. They say something like, "The teacher asked me a question about an important national monument," and you answer, "So, what happened after they asked you this question?" Then, after letting your grandchild talk for a while, you can summarize the conversation by texting something like, "It sounds like you're upset about the grade your teacher gave you. Am I right?"

When you talk to someone face-to-face, you display your active listening skills by using minimal encouragers like "Mhmm," Wow," or "Really?" Thanks to these simple words, you show them that you listen to them carefully without interrupting their thoughts. When you write a message on social media platforms, you can take advantage of emojis or use the same words you would use in real-life conversations. For instance, if someone tells you something that surprises you, you can use the face screaming in fear that you discovered in Chapter 3 to express shock. Last but not least, the most important tool for practicing active listening in online interactions is open-ended questions. When people send messages, they tend to be very quick and provide simple answers like "Okay" or "Yes." However, you can enhance your conversations in the digital world by asking open-ended questions, thus making the interactions last longer. If your grandchild tells you that they got a low grade, avoid saying something like, "Oh, I'm so sorry!" Instead, ask them how they feel or what they plan to do in the future to get a better grade.

### *Amplifying Your Listening Skills*

Understanding active listening skills and following some practical tips is paramount to enhance your empathy and learn to communicate with younger generations, but they might not be enough. The real problem with instant messaging and online interactions is that everything happens rapidly, and people expect you to provide a quick answer to their messages. How can you overcome this obstacle? You can learn something from the world of improvised comedy, which involves making people laugh by inventing things in the moment and reacting to stimuli that occur in the here and now. When comedians improvise, they don't think about their jokes before going on stage but let them arise as they interact with the public and become aware of the environment and atmosphere. In other words, they use their listening skills to grasp what's happening around them and respond appropriately to make the audience laugh. As you might guess, improvising is hard, but that's exactly what you do when you text someone. In fact, the most important skill you must develop is listening.

Improvised comedians improve their listening skills by repeating some useful exercises that you can try yourself while answering texts. Don't worry—they're very easy, and you can practice them with your grandchildren when they send you messages on WhatsApp or other apps. The first exercise simply involves repeating the same words used by the other person. For instance, let's say one of your grandchildren text you that next summer, they want to visit New York. Your conversation might go like this:

- "I want to go to New York."
- "New York? Why?"
- "Because I want to see Central Park."
- "Ah, Central Park is beautiful. I've never seen it."
- "Would you like to come with me?"
- "Come with you? I don't know."

And so on. This way, the conversation goes smoothly while you repeat one or more words used by your grandchild. Moreover, you answer promptly without taking a lot of time to reflect on what to say or writing too much, thus losing their attention.

Another exercise that you can try with your grandchildren is to invent stories using one word at a time. Such activities are extremely funny for Gen Z members, as they enjoy the type of humor that might derive from them and are used to gamification, as you learned in previous chapters. Before starting, tell them that your story will begin with "Once upon a time," and then, everyone can say whatever they want—they just have to send one message at a time with only one word. Decide who starts the exercise and have fun. The final result should look something like this:

- Once
- Upon
- A
- Time
- I
- Went
- To
- Edinburgh
- To
- Meet
- A
- Magician

As you can see from the example, you can write down whatever you can think of, even if it doesn't make sense or isn't real. This is a good way of bonding with your grandchildren while having fun together.

Accepting that the world has changed and things are different is complicated but necessary if you want to build a strong and deep connection with younger generations. To reduce the generation gap and understand your grandchildren, you must build empathy and active listening skills. This way, you learn to put yourself in their shoes and become aware of what they need and want. In this chapter, we started discussing tone and context and how misunderstandings can easily arise online. In the next one, we'll dive deep into the topic of discord and learn how to deal with conflicts online effectively.

# CHAPTER 6

# THE DIGITAL DE-ESCALATION HANDBOOK

## BOOMER TECHNIQUES FOR TURNING DISCORD INTO DISCOURSE

> *The ultimate measure of a man is not where he stands in moments of comfort and convenience, but where he stands at times of challenge and controversy.*

— MARTIN LUTHER KING, JR.

The digital world is a jungle where you interact with people with different backgrounds and opinions, so it's easy to get lost and take the wrong path. Moreover, remember that the absence of essential cues to interpret others' words leads to more misunderstandings and misinterpretations. This means that conflicts can rapidly arise and escalate, and you might get trapped in a storm of aggression and negative language. How can you avoid such situations? In the following sections, you'll discover how online arguments work, how to engage in productive online debate, and how to de-escalate a dangerous conflict. Next, you'll learn strategies to find common ground with the people you argue with, avoid arguments completely, and deal with heated conflicts.

## LOOKING INTO THE EYE OF THE STORM: DISSECTING ONLINE CONFLICT

People use social media to do a variety of things, especially connecting with loved ones and people all over the world. Although conversations are usually harmless, arguments can easily arise and become heated. Everything starts with someone expressing their opinion on a specific topic and another one replying, opposing their point of view, and asking for proof of their ideas.

The person who expressed their opinion in the first place immediately feels attacked and tries their best to make their voice heard and demonstrate that they're right, thus producing evidence that supports their ideas. The second person usually doesn't consider the information accurate and trustworthy and dismisses the first person's opinion, integrating their point of view with additional information and articles that support their ideas. Without even realizing it, the two people enter an infinite loop where they keep telling each other that they're right and their opinion is correct while their opponent is wrong. Potentially, the argument can go on for hours without reaching a compromise or finding a middle ground.

Conflicts online are common for various reasons, the most evident one being that some people like provoking arguments. However, the situation is much more complicated than that, as statistics and research show. Studies have found that conflicts arise more easily on social media platforms like WhatsApp and Facebook, while YouTube and Instagram are basically argument-free. When arguing on WhatsApp, people feel free to express their point of view honestly and are more open to finding a compromise. In contrast, when they argue on Facebook, they're aware that their friends and followers are "watching" them, and they don't feel comfortable being authentic and sincere (Baughan, 2021).

The main difference is that conflicts on WhatsApp arise in private chats where people know each other and maintain their focus on the problem at hand, while on Facebook, they know others are watching, so they want to prove they're right and win over their opponents. This means that people use social media platforms differently, and their design influences their reactions. In fact, people don't argue on YouTube a lot because they focus on watching videos, and when they leave a comment, it's mainly to provide feedback on what they see and not oppose someone's ideas from the start (Baughan, 2021).

In addition to all of that, social media has an incredible effect on our mental health and pushes us to keep scrolling and commenting, thus prolonging conflicts. Platforms are designed to keep us engaged, so we feel the urge to use them as much as we can. Therefore, we struggle to end arguments, even when they're heated and senseless. Moreover, people behave differently than in real life. According to many researchers, we're more likely to engage in negative behaviors and use rude and offensive language online because we don't experience the same inhibitions we have offline (3 *Reasons People Argue Online*, 2020).

When arguing in our real lives, we must be brave enough to say what we want to say in someone's face, which is extremely hard for most of us. Conversely, the internet allows us to argue with whomever we want without even looking them in the face or having a chance to see them in real life. Therefore, we feel entitled to use demeaning language. At the same time, we're all subjected to biases and prejudices that determine our reactions, and they become evident in online conflicts. If someone criticizes our ideas, we feel compelled to defend ourselves because we take our truth for granted and are 100% sure we're right. As the other person holds the same belief, we would both do whatever is necessary to prove ourselves and win the argument. However, such behaviors only make the situation worse.

Engaging in online conflicts has many negative effects not only on your online interactions and relationships but also on your mental and physical health. In fact, research has found that engaging in arguments online is as bad as experiencing burnout and has real-life impacts. For example, you might feel more anxious every time you use social media and don't feel free to post or comment on anything for fear of others' reactions. Consequently, you feel more stressed, thus hindering all aspects of your life, not only your online interactions. At the same time, you keep replaying the same conversations over and over or thinking about how to reply to someone's comment, running the risk of developing insomnia. Finally, you might incur physical disorders like high blood pressure, diabetes, or ulcers (Stone, 2021). As you can see, engaging in arguments online only has negative effects on your mental and physical health and personal life.

## HOW TO ENGAGE IN PROPER ONLINE DEBATE

When you start using your social media accounts, you might want to share your opinions on specific topics, articles, and sources that you find interesting and worth sharing with your online friends. After some time, you check your post and notice that most of your followers liked it or left a positive comment about your opinion, except for one. They didn't like what you shared and felt the urge to express their opinion in front of all your friends. Without even realizing it, you might be stuck in an argument with this follower, trying to prove your point. As happens in these occasions, helpers or opponents might intervene and agree or disagree with you, thus making the conflict even more difficult to handle.

How can you engage in similar situations without losing your mind or spending hours and hours on social media, replying to comments? Well, you can follow some simple rules. When you share something, make sure to be clear, concise, and precise to avoid misinterpretations and misunderstandings. If a debate arises, follow the same process to increase the possibility that the other person understands your words and what you mean. When you're in the middle of an argument, you might be tempted to react impulsively and write the first thing you can think of, but it will likely be counterproductive and make the argument more heated. Instead, take a few seconds after reading comments and clear your mind before writing anything so that you have an objective perspective and don't take things personally. At the same time, if you notice that the other person is unclear or you don't understand what they mean, avoid assuming and just ask them what they mean.

To engage in online debate properly, you must also focus on ideas and not people. When talking about politics, it's easy to lose your focus on the main topic and start talking about politicians instead of what they do. Consequently, you can start a discussion about immigration and end up comparing Biden and Trump. Such conversations are fruitless and can get personal rapidly, as people feel closer to politicians than the politics they enact. If you notice that someone concentrates on people rather than ideas in their speech, divert their attention back to the problem. The same is true when you talk to someone online and criticize their personal characteristics instead of their ideas. Saying something like, "You're wrong," creates a different response in others than saying, "I think your ideas are wrong." People feel attacked personally when others criticize their traits and themselves as individuals. Conversely, they're more prone to open and productive discussion if they notice that only their opinions are criticized.

Another common pitfall of online debates is insults. People tend to show their worst online and are more likely to insult or demean you for your opinion. In response, you might be tempted to insult them back, maybe even wittily, but this can only lead to negative outcomes. The great advantage of online conflicts is that you can avoid replying to some comments, so just ignore insults and move on. In addition, remember that you always have an exit plan to stop the conversation whenever you feel like it. If others keep commenting, you don't have to reply. The most effective way of escaping from an endless and useless argument is to write something like, "I enjoyed chatting with you, but for me, it's time to leave this conversation because it's taking up too much of my time, as I'm sure it's the same for you. Thank you." By using these words, you show respect, which might prompt the other person to stop the argument peacefully, too.

## DE-ESCALATING TENSE ONLINE CONVERSATIONS

The tips in the above section are certainly helpful but might not be enough to support you in tough moments, especially when conversations become tense. This happens to everyone, as we all get blown away by arguments and might not be able to stay calm when someone insults us or demeans our ideas. In such cases, you have the power to de-escalate the situation to avoid transforming the discussion into a heated conflict.

First, you must reflect on yourself and your emotions. Take a few moments to think about how you feel and why you should shift your focus to yourself rather than the person you're debating with. The key to de-escalating conflicts is to stay calm and use clear and precise language, as you learned previously. Therefore, take all the time you need to gather your thoughts, analyze your emotions, and relax. If you want, just take your eyes away from your computer screen or smartphone for some time or even put them aside. Then, take a walk in your house or outside to concentrate on something else that is more connected to your real world.

When you feel ready, pick up your phone or computer and leave an honest and respectful comment to model calm behavior and encourage the other person to do the same. Whatever they say to you, just stay calm and take all the time to consider your replies before writing them down. An effective way of defusing an argument also involves validating their feelings and thoughts and trying to understand their point of view. Show interest in their opinion and ask them more about it: where it came from, how, and why. Try to put yourself in their shoes and use sentences like, "I can understand why this topic makes you feel upset," or "You have every reason to be angry." Help them realize that their feelings and thoughts are normal and okay.

When you find yourself in the middle of a tense debate, you might be tempted to just run away, close all your social media, and stop looking at it for a while. However, flying away from one moment to another might make the other person even angrier, and the argument might escalate even more. For this reason, spend as much time as you can validating their emotions and thoughts and maintaining a calm attitude. When you notice they appear a bit more relaxed, take the opportunity to respectfully end the conversation.

Below, you will find examples of sentences you can use to defuse an argument:

- How do you feel?
- Thanks for raising this issue; I think it took guts.
- I respect your point of view. Here's what I think.
- What do you need right now?
- Your opinion derives from a very different perspective, so it's natural that we think differently.
- I think you said this thing; am I correct?
- How can I make you feel better?
- Let's take a break until we feel more relaxed and keep talking about this topic later, okay?
- Do we really need to agree on this issue?

## FINDING COMMON GROUND

When arguments arise, the goal is to find common ground, which is a specific topic or opinion you and the other person agree to. Even when you think you're completely different from them, there's always something you share with them—

no matter how insignificant it looks. To find common ground, focus on your similarities and the things you agree about. For example, you might have different opinions on climate change. Still, I'm sure you both agree that protecting the environment is important, and we all want to leave a better place for future generations. By finding common ground, you create a deeper connection with them and improve the chances of ending the conflict effectively.

You must also try to understand the other person's point of view and see things from their perspective. Keep in mind that there's always a reason behind every thought and opinion, and, in most cases, it is valid. Try to investigate why they have a different opinion on the topic and put yourself in their shoes. For instance, they might be in favor of stricter rules concerning immigration because they're afraid they'd lose their job due to migrants. As you might guess, this fear is big and might lead to having harsh opinions about immigration. Acknowledge that losing a job is always difficult and daunting and that you understand their emotions. Then, explain your position respectfully.

In the previous chapter, you learned about active listening, which is a powerful skill. You can put it into practice during conflicts to focus on the other person's point of view and pay more attention to listening to them rather than proving a point so that you're more likely to find common ground. Moreover, remember that every opinion counts and makes the world a better place, even if it's hard to believe. If we all agreed with each other, we would never innovate and evolve as a species, and we would never discover new things to try. By having different opinions, we challenge ourselves. We are more likely to reconsider our ideas and see things from a different perspective, thus enriching our vision of the world and ourselves. If you start an argument with someone, avoid seeing it as a way of proving your point but as an opportunity to learn from someone who has different beliefs and comes from a different background.

## AVOIDING CONFLICT IN THE FIRST PLACE

In addition to dealing with conflicts effectively, you can also avoid them in the first place. In fact, you can choose if, how, and when you want to engage online and must use this power to your advantage. The most effective strategy to avoid arguments is identifying them before they arise. If you post something online and someone leaves a negative comment or says something inappropriate, avoid the temptation to immediately reply. Sometimes, the best thing to do to avoid conflicts is simply never start engaging with them.

If someone criticizes you or your ideas, just let them say what they want and don't reply to their comments. This way, you'll easily defuse the argument without saying a word. Remember that the person with the greatest strength is not the one who spends all day replying to all comments but the one who decides when and how to engage in arguments. Try not to reply to a negative comment and see how the other person responds. In the beginning, they might feel the urge to direct your attention toward them, thus leaving more comments or becoming more aggressive. However, as they notice that you never reply to them, they lose their interest and stop bothering you.

Avoiding conflicts online requires some practice because you must get used to identifying those who argue just for the sake of it, otherwise known as trolls. Trolls are people who leave comments because they want to intentionally provoke a negative reaction in you through insults, harassment, and other forms of unhealthy behavior. To avoid trolls, learn to understand if someone is texting you in good faith or wants to induce an online conflict. You can easily spot them by paying attention to the words they use. If they're in good faith, they're more likely to use a respectful tone of voice and express their opinion honestly without insulting yours. If they're not, they probably don't provide any resources or information to back up their opinion and focus on attacking and demeaning you rather than having a constructive debate. If you notice that a troll left you a comment, follow the advice above and simply don't fuel their desire to provoke arguments, so never reply.

Finally, you have the power to avoid conflicts by reflecting on the things you want to post online. If you think that a comment could be controversial and cause heated debates among your followers, avoid sharing it on your social media. Keep in mind that some topics can be easily discussed face-to-face and are more suited for real-life, private conversations. Therefore, choose your posts and words carefully and select the content you want to share.

## CALMING HACKS FOR THOSE HEATED ONLINE MOMENTS

Dealing with conflicts online is not easy because you must stay calm and focus on understanding the other person's point of view instead of proving you're right. In the above sections, you found useful strategies to de-escalate arguments and avoid them. Below, you find some useful hacks to remember when you need to calm down and deal with conflicts online.

- **Build bridges:** Throughout the chapter, we talked about practicing active listening and validating the other person's feelings and thoughts. In the end, everything involves building bridges and focusing on the similarities instead of the differences. Try to be empathetic and focus on the fact that they're another human being and have needs and wants like everyone else. If you find points of connection with them, you're more likely to achieve positive outcomes and end the conflict effectively.
- **Watch for cues of escalation:** Remember that emotions play a crucial role in the conclusion of an argument, so try to manage them and focus on

the topic at hand. At a certain point of a conflict, you might notice that you feel threatened: Your breathing shortens, and your heart rate increases. As soon as you identify these signs, acknowledge that you're losing control and it's time to take a few seconds to calm down.

- **Analyze your anger:** The most common feeling during arguments is anger because you feel attacked by someone who criticizes your ideas, as happens to many of us. Understanding your anger is paramount to controlling your reactions and not reacting impulsively. Accept that it's a normal emotion we all feel from time to time, and you have every right to be angry at someone. Instinctively, you might repress your anger and keep it inside you or act on it and be aggressive toward the other person. Instead, discover where this emotion comes from to understand what exactly makes you feel that way and provokes unwanted reactions.

- **Have a laugh:** Focusing and acting on negative emotions during an argument is easy and common, but it's not the most productive way of handling conflicts. Conversely, expressing positive feelings and bringing some light to the conversation can change the outcomes and bring you closer to the other person. In particular, laughs have the incredible power of boosting your mood and making you see things from a new perspective. If you laugh with the person you're arguing with, you create a connection, thus feeling more empathetic toward them and being more likely to find common ground. For example, if you notice that you make a grammar mistake in a text, use your sense of humor to laugh about it. Alternatively, find the funny side of a topic and talk about it with the other person.

The reasons why conflicts arise online are numerous and mainly revolve around the design of social media platforms and the desire of some people to provoke arguments just for the fun of it. Some platforms, like WhatsApp and Facebook, are more likely to cause conflicts, so be careful while using them. The key to dealing with arguments effectively is to listen to the other person carefully and understand their point of view. The more things you share, the more likely you are to solve the argument effectively. In fact, you must find common ground with the person you're arguing with to create a connection. In this chapter, we mentioned the importance of being respectful and using positive language. In the next one, we'll dive deep into this topic by discussing online etiquette and strategies to be safe.

# CHAPTER 7

# ONLINE CLASS

## A GUIDE TO STAYING POLITE (AND PROTECTED) ONLINE

A s you learned in Chapter 1, the internet is an intricate web of computers connected around the world that share data all the time. Whatever you do online passes through these computers and is saved. As the internet is vast and complicated, it's hard to imagine how and when your information and activity are stored, but it is. That's why you might have probably heard that the internet is forever: Whatever you do online stays there indefinitely. When you post something, you have the power to delete it, but you must be careful. For example, if you stop using Facebook but don't delete your account, your activity on this social media platform will stay visible to everyone all the time, even if someone wants to see your profile in 10 or 20 years.

Deleting content that you don't want others to see gives you the power to control your online activity, but it might not be enough. In fact, your friends and followers can handle your posts however they want. They can share them, save them on their smartphones or computers, or screenshot them (which means that they take pictures of your posts). When they possess this information, they can do whatever they want with it. That's why the internet is considered a dangerous place, and it's important to know how to protect yourself online.

In the next sections, you'll learn about netiquette—digital etiquette—and how to use it to have positive and healthy interactions with others online. Next, you'll discover how to set online boundaries to stay safe and ways to protect your privacy. Finally, you'll find some useful tips and strategies to practice online safety and the most common dangers you should know about and avoid.

## NETIQUETTE 101: HOW NOT TO CROSS THE LINE WHEN YOU'RE ONLINE

The word "netiquette" derives from the combination of "internet" and "etiquette" and concerns the manners and healthy behaviors we should engage in while navigating online. It became necessary when people started interacting more online and noticed that, as we all need rules in our real lives, we also need them in the digital world. The core or golden rules of netiquette were first introduced by author Virginia Shea in 1994 in her book *Core Rules of Netiquette*. The main idea behind these rules was to create a standard of polite behavior all internet users should maintain to have healthy and positive interactions online. Since 1994, the rules have been adjusted and improved based on the latest technological advancements, especially the development of social media platforms. Thanks to them, you protect yourself from online dangers, develop a positive online image, and improve your communication skills on the internet (Menguin, 2023).

But what are these golden rules? Here's the list:

- Remember that there's a human being behind every screen, so behave with empathy and respect.
- Make sure to use clear, concise, and simple language to ensure that everyone understands your point of view and doesn't misinterpret or misunderstand your words.
- Behave in online places as you would in offline ones. When you talk to your friends about gardening tips offline, for example, you don't demean others' opinions or state that their techniques are obvious or useless. When you're online, you might be tempted to act this way, as you don't see them in person, and feel free to express your unfiltered opinion. However, that's not what netiquette asks of you. As you're kind and respectful offline, so you must be online. Therefore, thank your friends for their tips and move on.
- Respect others' privacy as you would like them to do with you. For instance, if one of your family members sends you a private message, keep it private and avoid sharing it in WhatsApp groups or other social media platforms.

- When you notice any form of misbehavior, like bullying, immediately report it to the relevant platform so that they can do something about it.
- Ask for permission before using someone else's content. When you navigate online, you can find plenty of pictures, videos, and images that you might want to share on your social media profiles. Just keep in mind that all that content comes from somewhere: Someone made it and shared it online. Therefore, ask for their permission before using their content.
- Respect cultural and personal differences, as you'll find many different people online who have different backgrounds.
- Pay attention to grammar and spelling and check them before posting something or texting someone.
- Avoid sharing content that might be considered hateful or offensive to maintain online positivity.
- Remember that everything you do online leaves a trail, so think twice before sharing any content.

### Direct Messages

The above golden rules apply to all online situations, but you might need to behave differently according to the platform or communication channel you're using. For instance, direct messages (DMs) allow you to send private texts to a specific person, and nobody except you two can read them. You have DMs on all social media platforms and can use them to deepen your connection with someone and engage in longer and more detailed conversations. However, you must keep in mind some essential rules, the first one being that you should think before sending any message, even if it's private. When we text in public, we filter our reactions because we know our friends and followers are watching us. However, in DMs, we might be tempted to be less respectful, thus hindering our communication and online interactions. To avoid such situations, ask yourself the following question before sending a message: *Would I share this information publicly, or would I say the same thing on my profile where everyone can see it?* If the answer is "No," then you shouldn't write about it in DMs either.

When you talk to someone in private, you must also remember not to correct their grammar or spelling mistakes unless they ask you to because it's not polite to emphasize others' errors. In addition, be careful of the time you choose to send a DM to someone. For example, I suggest you avoid texting late at night because it might have negative effects on the receiver's mental health, especially if you want to send a difficult message. As grammar and spelling are paramount, so is sentence structure. Avoid texting one simple word with exclamation or question marks, but phrase your questions and thoughts so that the receiver clearly understands what you want from them. Finally, keep in mind that nobody owes anything online. If someone shares posts, pictures, and videos, it doesn't mean they owe you more content or more detailed information. Accept what they decide to share, and don't ask them to share more or help you with specific requests. This is especially true with bloggers, influencers, and similar professional figures.

## Social Media Posts

When you post something on your social media accounts, everybody can see it—not only now but for the years and decades to come. That's why you must pay attention to the content you share online and make sure that it aligns with your offline identity. If you're kind and generous offline, be the same online. In other words, make your posts authentic so that they mirror your personality and the things you like in the real world, too. At the same time, authenticity is considered essential online, which means that your friends and followers will appreciate it more and be more likely to leave positive comments and react positively to your posts.

When you post something, focus not only on what you share but on the people who react to your content. If you dedicate time to answering others' comments politely and ask them more questions to investigate what they truly enjoy about your content, you show genuine care and interest, which is a good quality to have online. People will understand you care about them, and you'll be able to build stronger and deeper relationships.

Moreover, avoid oversharing to protect your privacy and not deal with conflicts and misunderstandings. Oversharing is the act of sharing too much personal information about your location, work, and future plans, as well as your thoughts, inner feelings, and concerns. The more you share online, the more you risk that people will use it against you. For example, bad people might use your personal information to know your moves and steal valuable things from you, or someone might react negatively to your feelings and thoughts, thus making you feel even worse and hindering your mental health.

## Comments

If someone replies to one of your posts or you see an interesting discussion online, you might want to participate and leave a comment. Before saying anything, make sure to read the original post carefully and check all the previous comments to avoid repetitions. When you read comments about a hot topic, you might lose control and let your emotions decide your next moves, but that's not healthy. Instead, take a few seconds to reflect on the post and previous comments and provide an adequate answer.

In addition, pay attention to the language and tone of voice to align your replies to previous ones. If you notice that the conversation runs smoothly and everyone is being respectful and honest, do the same. Conversely, if you notice that someone leaves a negative comment under one of your posts and a conflict arises, ask yourself what your role might be and how the content you shared might have provoked such reactions. Reflecting on your posts allows you to become more self-aware and understand what's best to share online.

## PRIVACY AND BOUNDARIES IN THE DIGITAL AGE

Boundaries are paramount in all relationships, both in the online and offline world. Boundaries are limits you set while interacting with others to feel comfortable with your inner self and the people around you. When you set healthy boundaries, you enhance your mental and physical health and build stronger and more positive relationships because you know what you want and need from others, and they respect you for who you are. An example of a healthy boundary might be to let your partner know that you don't feel comfortable inviting all their family to dinner every Sunday because you prefer relaxing on the couch, watching some TV on your own. Healthy boundaries are important online, too, because they identify your limits when interacting with others on social media platforms.

How can you set healthy online boundaries? Start by acknowledging that you have the power to say "No," like you have in your real life. Therefore, you don't have to befriend every stranger who sends you a request to become your friend on Facebook or put a like in every post on your best friend's account. Remember to be authentic and only do the things you feel comfortable with. Moreover, think about why you use social media and keep your purpose in mind in all the activities you complete. Do you want 400 friends on Facebook, or do you just really need your loved ones? How much personal information do you want to share in your profile? How many followers do you want to have on your social media accounts? Another tip you must follow to set healthy boundaries is to check and adjust the time you spend online. Nobody is immune to the incredible power of social media, which keeps us online for hours and hours every day. Just like your grandchildren might struggle to stop scrolling, so might you. Keep track of the time you spend online and take control of it by deciding how much time you want to spend surfing the internet.

The concept of online boundaries is strictly connected with privacy, which is the right to be free from unwanted disclosure of personal information. If you respect your and others' privacy, you don't share personal information without the consent of the person who is directly involved, don't over-share on your social media profiles, don't send unsolicited messages, and respect privacy settings. By respecting others' privacy, you build healthier online relationships and protect yourself more effectively. In particular, privacy settings allow you to decide how much personal information you want to share and with whom. If you're curious to see your privacy settings, just open one of your social media accounts (you'll find them in all social media), search for the settings, and look for the word "Privacy." You'll notice that, for example, all platforms give you the opportunity to have a private or public profile. If you have a private profile, it means that only your friends and followers can access the content you share. This way, you protect yourself from malicious people who want to use your information inappropriately.

In addition to setting a private profile, you can choose what you want to share with your followers and other people on social media. For instance, you can decide that only your closest friends or followers can see specific posts, or people who don't follow you aren't allowed to leave comments on your posts. Due to recent scandals, tech companies give much importance to privacy and make sure you have control over your content and what you want to share. Use this power to protect yourself and ensure others don't use your personal information without your consent.

## ONLINE SAFETY

Online safety involves protecting yourself from the risks and harms that might result in unsafe communication, scams, stolen information, or physical and mental harm. As you've probably heard, the internet is a dangerous place, and not everyone has good intentions: Some people might text you because they want to take your money, while others might want to hinder your mental health by criticizing you and your opinion. If you look at recent statistics, the situation is alarming. From 2015 to

2020, six million people experienced cyber threats, and an online attack occurs every 39 seconds. Moreover, almost 100 million people in 20 countries were affected by cybercrime in 2017, and one in ten Americans reported severe forms of harassment online. Last but not least, every month, more than 300,000 malicious websites are detected by authorities (Lindner, 2023). These are just some of the statistics that refer to people not being safe online.

However, this doesn't mean that you should never use the internet or create social media accounts. Conversely, being aware of the most common online dangers and understanding how they work allows you to stay safe online and take the necessary measures to protect yourself. The more you're aware of what happens online, the more you can avoid difficult or dangerous situations. You might believe that the most vulnerable targets of online danger are children, and that's not completely false, as many people try to take advantage of them in one way or another. However, as an adult, you're not completely immune.

Among all the dangers you might incur, scams are arguably the most popular ones. Scams are frauds invented by people who mainly want to steal your money. They can work in different ways, but their strategy usually involves messages or calls that tell you to send money to a specific bank account you've never heard of. Those who invent scams are called scammers, and they can use whatever information they know about you, even tell you that your grandchildren are in danger and need your money as soon as possible to be safe. Whenever something similar happens to you, remember that no authentic and legit authority, organization, or person would ask you to send them your bank account or other personal information related to your money. Therefore, never send anything.

Another form of online scam is called phishing, which refers to people who pose as legitimate governmental institutions and ask you for money. For instance, a bank you don't have a bank account with might send you a message saying that you need to update or change your PIN in some way. In all cases, these are frauds, and you shouldn't send any information.

Another prevalent danger is known as hacking, which is perpetrated by so-called hackers, who are people with excellent technical computer skills who breach cybersecurity defenses. Hackers operate in many different ways and might attack both individuals and companies. One of the tools they usually use is viruses. They install a virus in your computer by pushing you to click on a link or do similar actions. Once you click, the virus is on your computer or smartphone, and they can access and use your personal information against you. Hackers are very dangerous and might be able to possess very sensitive information that affects your bank accounts and personal life.

Finally, another common danger is fake news, which is news that looks legitimate but is actually false. The main problem with them is that you might believe they correspond to reality, so you share them, thus spreading false information online and hindering your online reputation and persona. As a non-digital native, you're more susceptible to false news because you struggle to identify the difference between a trustworthy and real source of information and a false one.

That's absolutely normal and happens to all of us—even the youngest ones.

How can you stay safe online? Follow the tips below!

- **Create strong passwords:** When you have multiple social media accounts and subscribe to different websites, you automatically have to create numerous passwords. Many people decide to use the same one on different websites to save time, but this is not safe. If someone hacks into one of your accounts, it's very likely that they'll have access to other accounts, too. When creating a password, make it as strong as possible by using upper and lower case letters, symbols, and numbers. Moreover, avoid using personal information (like your name, surname, or date of birth) or simple words (like "password"), which are easy to track. The more unique your password is, the fewer the chances of it being deciphered by someone. In general, I would recommend creating a password of at least 10 or 12 characters so that it's strong enough.

- **Enhance your network security:** The network you use plays a crucial role in your safety. When you're at home, you probably use your Wi-Fi, which is password-protected and increases your safety. When you connect to a network outside your house, you might connect to your local bar or restaurant Wi-Fi, which is usually free and accessible by anyone, thus being less secure. When you go out, avoid using unprotected networks to ensure no one steals your data online.

- **Beware of hackers:** Among the tricks hackers use to access your personal information, one of the most popular is making you click where you shouldn't. While navigating online, you might be redirected to pages that tell you that you've won an incredible amount of money or you're one of the luckiest people in the world. The rule of thumb is to carefully read the message you receive. If it's too good to be true and you didn't do anything in particular to earn that money, then it's a scam. Consequently, avoid sending personal information or clicking on buttons like "I'm the winner," "Get your money now," or "Download this app." Moreover, pay attention to the emails you receive, as that's one of hackers' favorite channels. If you don't know the sender, don't open the email at all or do some research to find out more about them before replying.

- **Use firewall protection:** Firewalls and antivirus software protections keep you safe from simple scams and fraud, so it's better to install one on your computer and smartphone. Consider the previous example of a web page that tells you that you won a lot of money: Firewalls disable it and don't allow you to take any action except closing the page, thus protecting you from clicking a dangerous link.

- **Close accounts you don't use:** Keep track of all the accounts you open online and close the ones you don't need anymore. Keep in mind that they contain your personal information, and if you don't check them regularly, hackers might access them without you being aware and steal or misuse your data.

- **Make sure that the website you're visiting is safe:** Another strategy hackers use to steal your information is leading you to unsafe websites to make you insert personal data and save it. To check if a website is safe, you can follow some easy tips. First, check the URL in the address bar at the top of your web browser. If the URL starts with "https:/" and ends with the symbol of a lock, it means that it's secure. Moreover, international laws force websites to have a web page that discusses their privacy policy. If the one you're navigating doesn't have one or doesn't clearly explain how your privacy is protected, then it's not legit. Another good way of checking if a website is safe is to read its reviews online. Just type its name on the Google search bar and write "reviews:" If all the reviews are extremely positive or they're all bad, it's very likely that the website isn't real or safe. Moreover, check for grammar, spelling, design mistakes, and contact information. If a website isn't well-written, or it's hard to navigate, and it doesn't provide any contact information about its managers, it's probably unsafe.

Staying safe and protecting your privacy online is hard work but necessary to ensure a positive and healthy experience with digital tools and social media. If you learn to use netiquette, you take the first steps toward protecting yourself and ensuring positive online interactions. However, you also need to check your privacy settings, be aware of common online dangers, and apply the necessary safety tips. At this point, the only thing left to do is strengthen your online relationships and, maybe, deepen them in the real world. In the next chapter, you'll learn everything about cultivating online and offline connections.

# CHAPTER 8

# BYTE-SIZED BONDS

## CULTIVATING CONNECTIONS WITH THE YOUNGER GENERATIONS

D id you know that the first video call was officially made in 1927 and that this new technology was considered a flop for decades? The company AT&T had monopolistic control of the U.S. phone services and took advantage of its position to launch video calls, but it was never successful. The idea of seeing someone while speaking to them from somewhere far away didn't grab people's attention and interest. In 1993, a breakthrough was made by a scientist from the University of Cambridge who gave birth to the webcams as we know them today. From that moment, services like Skype were born and developed as people wanted webcams installed on their computers. When Apple CEO Steve Jobs launched the iPhone 4 and introduced FaceTime in 2010, the revolution officially started, and video calls became more and more common among people. Thanks to FaceTime, we can video call others not only from our computers but also from our smartphones (Uenuma, 2020).

Nowadays, video calls are a fundamental tool to keep in touch and interact with others all over the world. They're just one of the numerous ways to build deep connections with younger generations, especially your grandchildren. In the upcoming sections, you'll discover the importance of connecting with them and strategies to balance offline and online interactions to develop a strong relationship with them. Finally, you'll learn useful tips to disconnect from all technologies every now and then to maintain good mental health.

## WHY IT MATTERS TO CONNECT WITH THE YOUNG ONES AS A YOUNG ONCE

Human beings are social animals, so we're hard-wired to connect with the people around us and can't live without interacting with others. That's because social connections have incredible benefits for our mental and physical health and enrich not only us but also the people with whom we connect. In other words, social connections are based on giving and receiving at the same time. By interacting with others, we boost our mood, especially when we connect with younger ones. If you have grandchildren, you certainly witness their effect on your mental and physical health, as they keep you young at heart and help you see reality from different and new points of view. By seeing things through their eyes, you re-evaluate the world around you and are amazed by all the beauty that surrounds you.

By interacting with younger generations, you also feel less lonely and excluded because you develop deeper connections. On one hand, you feel more hopeful and enthusiastic because you experience your grandchildren's incredible energy and feel closer to them. On the other hand, you offer them your wisdom, thus teaching them important life lessons. At the same time, you have the opportunity to learn new skills and explore the world from their perspective. By connecting with others, especially younger generations, you allow yourself to understand technological advancements and how to use modern digital tools like smartphones and social media. As your grandchildren learn from your stories and experiences, so do you from their excellent knowledge of new technologies as they guide you through the learning process and show you the steps you must take. If you think about it, your interactions with them are based on exchange and reciprocity.

Connecting with younger generations has many benefits not only for you but for your grandchildren, too, because they learn how the world worked before they were born and become aware of the process of aging, thus accepting it without problems. Thanks to your stories, you describe to them the world without smartphones and show them how things have changed in the last decades. You let them see that they are growing up in a different reality from you, and you explain the hardship and challenges you had to face at their age. When you tell them stories, you not only talk about your life but also pass on essential values and principles so that you give them the tools to navigate the world by themselves. In addition, you show them that there's nothing wrong with getting old and that you face these years with a positive attitude and an open mind. This way, you teach them to face the aging process peacefully. Moreover, building strong connections with younger generations allows you to reconsider your relationship with your children. Being a grandparent is different from being a parent, so you might see your kids differently and develop a deep connection through your interactions with your grandchildren.

Fostering social connections between you and younger generations has many more benefits, like improving your cognitive function, enhancing your empathy, and making you live a longer life. How is it possible? According to psychologist Maslow, there are five stages of needs: physiological, safety, love, esteem, and self-actualization. Physiological needs are the most basic ones, and we can't survive without them, so they're essential. Conversely, self-actualization needs aren't fundamental for our survival; instead, they increase our sense of self-fulfillment and make us feel happier and more satisfied with our lives. The needs of love and belonging constitute the third stage but are strictly connected with esteem and self-actualization because, without them, we can't achieve our full potential. As an elder, this is even more true: Research shows that increased social interactions improve your heart health and immune system, reduce the risk of depression and stress, and decrease the chances of developing dementia or Alzheimer's (Cockrell, 2022). These results show that even if the needs of love and belonging aren't considered essential for your survival, they have an incredible impact on other basic needs, such as good physical health.

As you can see, social interactions have incredible benefits for all of us, especially you, as you learn new skills and improve your overall well-being through building deep connections with your grandchildren and younger generations.

## ONLINE CONNECTIONS

To build strong and deep connections online, you must understand the difference between millennials and Gen Z. In the previous chapters, you already looked at fundamental differences and similarities between these two generations, but it's time to go a bit deeper and discover how you can build a profound rapport with them online.

When communicating, millennials prefer their smartphones over their computers and aren't used to sending a lot of emails because they tend to spend more time chatting with their friends and loved ones on social media platforms. Therefore, avoid sending them emails because they are unlikely to look at them or bother to answer you. They also prefer omnichannel experiences that allow them to connect with you on different levels, which is why they love social media. Thanks to it, they can send you a message instantly, share a post they like with you, and even video call you. One thing you must keep in mind is not to consider them as digital natives because that's not how they define themselves. In fact, they have a conflicting relationship with social media and other digital tools and aren't willing to absorb everything digitally. They might feel overwhelmed by digital interactions and disconnected from the real world, so you might want to build an offline connection, too, so that they feel safer and more relaxed.

If you want to connect with millennials online, remember that they all have a Facebook profile, but don't use it as much as you would expect. Conversely, they spend more time on platforms like Instagram, Pinterest, and Tumblr, so you might want to create an account on one of them. As you learned in Chapter 5, they don't like calls and prefer texting with their loved ones. Surprisingly, they're also the generation that uses social media more than any other, as they spend between 20 and 21 hours each month on social media platforms. They connect to the internet so often that they even use their smartphones while in the bathroom or at work (*Millennials: Technology = Social Connection*, 2014).

As for Gen Zs, they are heavily dependent on the internet because they've grown up with it, so they rely on it to complete all sorts of tasks, from interacting with friends and other people to buying clothes and having fun. If millennials enjoy texts more than calls, the same is valid for Gen Zs, or it's even more so. As they mainly communicate through social media platforms, they're used to instant messaging, so they avoid calling other people. Moreover, they consider themselves digital natives and are rightly so, as they were born when technologies were already prominent and part of everyone's daily life. Gen Zs are also experts in producing their own content and understanding when news is fake or a picture is not real, so pay attention to what you send them and check your sources before sending anything. This way, they acknowledge you understand how to use the internet and online information, thus valuing your point of view. In general, they give much importance to the truth and don't like being told fantasies, so you might want to stick to facts when interacting with them. Remember that they appreciate authenticity, so they don't need you to be their hero who accomplished everything without making any mistakes, but rather a normal person who has faced challenges and overcame them.

In addition, Gen Z aims to make a difference in the world, as you learned previously, so listen to them carefully and validate their feelings and thoughts to make them feel understood and loved for who they are. Don't criticize their ideas and dreams, but pay attention to their needs and wants and show them your support. If you want to interact with Gen Z, the most used social media platforms are YouTube, Snapchat, and Instagram. On YouTube, you don't have a chat where you can text them, but you can use other apps to send them interesting or funny videos to connect with them. Finally, remember that they have a short attention span, as you discovered in Chapter 4. This means that you must keep your texts, audio, and videos short to catch their attention and make them listen to you.

## OFFLINE CONNECTIONS

Although connecting online allows you to enter your grand-children's world and become aware of how social media works, you also need to build strong interactions in real life. Even if millennials and Gen Z spend most of their time looking at their smartphones, it doesn't mean that they don't need physical contact and be in touch with the world around them. Therefore, learn to use new technologies and social media but value offline connections, too.

The most important thing you must keep in mind is to be authentic, as that's what your grandchildren need from you. As a parent, you might have understood and accepted that you can't be perfect. As a grandparent, you might try not to make the same mistakes and appear amazing in front of your grandchildren's eyes. However, nobody is perfect, and they don't need you to always have all the answers and do the right thing. Conversely, they need you to be yourself and act authentically. This implies that you don't have to adapt your language and habits to them but simply be yourself. If you like reading books or gardening, show them how passionately you do such activities and pass on your interests to them. Moreover, acknowledge that your grandchildren might need practical life skills that smartphones and computers can't give them, like managing their own car, taking care of a pet, or organizing their daily routine. In such cases, you can be extremely helpful and teach them essential skills to prepare them for the real world.

Let's look at how you can connect with millennials and Gen Z offline. Millennials spend a lot of time on social media, but they value some quality time with friends and relatives. In particular, they enjoy playing old-fashioned board and trivia games, like Monopoly or Battleship. Challenge them to display their classic movie knowledge or scientific expertise to make things interesting for them and increase their engagement and fun with you. Millennials also enjoy doing things together, so invite them to your house to cook and have dinner together. In addition, they like learning new skills and expanding their knowledge. Alternatively, encourage them to spend some time away from their smartphones by going for a walk or watching a movie together. They'll certainly appreciate the precious moments with you. Millennials also spend most of their free time listening to music and watching YouTube videos, as recent statistics show (*The Top 10 Things Gen Z & Millennials Are Doing in Their Free Time*, 2022). To create a deep connection with them, ask them about their musical tastes and their favorite bands or singers and listen to their favorite songs. This way, you show interest in their free time and things they like doing and keep up to date with the latest songs.

Gen Zs also spend a lot of time on YouTube and listening to music, so you can connect with them through these channels. However, they also spend more time watching videos on social media platforms, which means that they like exchanging funny or interesting videos with their friends. If you create an Instagram or TikTok account, spend some time scrolling videos and thinking about which ones your grand-children might find interesting, then send one to them. In addition, Gen Zs enjoy playing video games more than millennials, so you might want to give them a try. They might appear complicated, like any other new technology, but they're also funny, engaging, and exciting. In addition to playing video games, Gen Zs also enjoy playing sports and value art, so you can accompany them to watch live sports or visit museums and art galleries—they'll surely appreciate your gesture. They're also more into dancing than millennials, probably because of the new social media platform TikTok, which is completely based on videos that people use to show dance moves and similar things. To create a connection with Gen Zs, you can try to show them how you used to dance at their age and what type of music you listened to.

## BALANCING DIGITAL AND FACE-TO-FACE INTERACTIONS FOR STRONGER BONDS

When you enter the world of social media, you might get trapped in it and struggle to connect to your real life and the people you interact with face-to-face every day. Social media is so powerful that it impacts your daily connections and can hinder your mental and physical health. For example, you might spend more time chatting with strangers on Facebook than talking to your neighbor, or you might spend your days scrolling social media, putting likes and hearts everywhere. As already mentioned, adults aren't immune to the negative effects of the internet, so we must all pay attention and keep track of the time we spend on social media.

To balance digital and face-to-face interactions, start by checking the time you spend on social media and limiting it based on your needs and wants. Let's say that six months ago, you installed Instagram and opened an account. In the last weeks, you noticed you spend about one hour every day scrolling it and putting hearts to pictures and videos that your followers share. Spending one hour of your time using social media might be too much, so check all the times you take your smartphone and try to reduce them. For instance, you might decide to look at your social media accounts only after lunch and dinner so that you considerably limit the time you spend on them. If you want, you can put a timer every time you open Instagram so that you're 100% sure you're dedicating the right amount to it. These tips are helpful for you and your grandchildren, so you can share them with them if you want.

Neglecting your real-life interactions might easily happen, especially if you're fascinated by all the people you find online. Suddenly, your neighbors and friends might appear not as interesting and funny as they used to be. However, building and maintaining offline connections is paramount for your overall well-being and allows you to stay connected to your true self and the real world. Therefore, make sure to schedule regular face-to-face interactions and focus on them. Since the arrival of the internet and social media, it might be hard to talk about something else, but you can give it a try with your old friends and other loved ones. When talking face-to-face, try to avoid discussions about social media and concentrate on the world around you and tangible things.

Last but not least, keep in mind that social media can improve or worsen your life depending on how you use and perceive it. If you immerse yourself in that world and let yourself get carried away by the latest trends, fake news, and similar things, you might hinder your mental and physical health and your offline and online relationships. Conversely, if you become aware of all the pros and cons of social media and how to use it properly—as you're learning in this book— you have the power to enhance your well-being and relationships. For instance, use social media to plan family gatherings and share your latest accomplishments but not to have a deep conversation with your children or grandchildren. In fact, I suggest you use such platforms to share funny or interesting pictures and videos and simply say "Hello" to your loved ones. However, I don't recommend you replace your offline interactions with instant messages and video calls because they're not the same, and they won't allow you to build a deep connection with younger generations.

## DOING A DIGITAL DETOX

Social media can be dangerous, so that's why you mustn't spend all your time using it. For this reason, many people consider doing a digital detox every once in a while to take some time away from the internet and everything that is online. You've probably heard about "detox," which is the shortening of "detoxification," a word that refers to the process of abstaining from or reducing the intake of toxins and unhealthy substances for our bodies. Digital tools aren't substances per se, but we all certainly need detoxification from them every now and then. If you want, you can do it with your grandchildren to share this experience and show them the importance of disconnecting from social media.

Research has found that taking a break from technology has incredibly positive effects on your mental and physical health. In fact, people feel less stressed and more relaxed because they don't feel the need to keep checking their emails and notifications. Moreover, their sleep quality and quantity improve because using social media before bedtime or while in bed increases insomnia and reduces sleep duration. In addition, those who practice detox feel an immediate boost in their mood and feelings as they develop a more positive life perspective (Cherry, 2020). How can you understand if you or one of your loved ones need a digital detox? The signs of spending too much time online are evident because you wake up in the morning and check your smartphone before doing anything else and go to bed doing the same thing before turning the light off. All your conversations revolve around things that happen online, like the latest trends and news, and you can't stay away from your smartphone for more than 15 minutes.

If you notice the above signs, it's time for a digital detox. There's no particular rule to follow except staying away from social media and the internet for some time, but you can follow some easy tips to make sure you take the appropriate actions. Turn off your smartphone every once in a while so that you're not tempted to look at it, especially before going to bed or while doing tasks that require your focus. If you have an iPhone, you also have the opportunity to turn notifications on and off as you please: You can decide when you want to receive calls from others during the day, when to receive notifications from social media apps, and when to answer WhatsApp messages. If you don't have an iPhone, you can still turn all your social media notifications off so that you don't look at your smartphone every time you receive one, but take it only when you feel like it.

Moreover, you can create no-phone areas in your house or even when you go outside. For example, the dinner table and bedroom might become no-phone areas, which means that you're not allowed to use your smartphones there. The same can be true when you go to your favorite bar or coffee shop so that you spend quality time enjoying the environment and watching the people around you. Another useful tip involves focusing on one screen at a time, which might be easy, but it's not, especially if you're used to multitasking. You might look at the TV and suddenly remember that you haven't texted your best friend in a while. Alternatively, you might try to understand how your computer works while texting your grandchildren. Focusing on more screens at the same time reduces your concentration, so it's better to avoid it. Finally, remember to keep only the most important things and get rid of the rest. When you enter the world of social media, you might download different apps and create numerous accounts to test different platforms. If, after a few weeks, you notice that you don't use some of them, simply delete them.

Finding the right balance between offline and online communication isn't easy. On one hand, the most effective way of interacting with younger generations is through social media, as this is their favorite communication channel. On the other hand, they need offline interactions to deepen their relationships and stay connected to the real world. Therefore, you must practice both social media and face-to-face activities to interact with them. However, pay attention to the time you spend on social media because it might hinder your mental and physical health, so do a digital detox every once in a while to enjoy your surroundings and remember that the offline world is just as amazing as the online one. At this point, you've explored various ways to bridge the gap between you and younger generations. Now, it's time to wrap up our discussion with some final thoughts on why these connections matter beyond the screens.

# WANT TO HELP OTHERS?

You may already be beginning to notice your connection with your grandchildren growing, and if not, you're close... and now you have a chance to help other grandparents do the same thing.

Simply by sharing your honest opinion of this book and a little about how it's helped you, you'll point new readers in the direction of the information they, too, are looking for.

Thank you so much for your support. May all your digital adventures be rewarding!

## Scan the QR code below

# CONCLUSION

If you think about it, the world has changed more in the last few decades than in the centuries before. Over the years, you've witnessed the evolution of the digital landscape, from TV and radio to AI. When you were young, you probably used to call your friends just to let them know you were available to go out, while right now, you might struggle to understand how to post a video on TikTok to show your followers how much you love your grandchildren. Such changes are so extraordinary that they're difficult to understand for everyone, even those who are supposed to be digital natives.

Throughout the book, you became aware of the main differences and similarities between three generations: baby boomers, millennials, and Gen Z. Baby boomers correspond to your generation and are the ones who struggle the most with keeping pace with the latest advancements and understanding how social media works. Millennials are identified as digital natives, but they actually have a contrasting relationship with technologies, as they both hate and love them. That's because they've witnessed most of the changes firsthand and had to adapt year after year. Finally, Gen Zs were born and grew up with social media and the latest digital tools, so they know how to use them effectively.

On one hand, these three generations have different relationships with technologies and seem distant from one another. On the other, they share some common concerns, doubts, values, and principles. Even if you struggle to understand social media, you can connect with younger generations by understanding the period when they grew up and recognizing that they want to connect with others and change the world just as much as you wanted to at their age. Even if they use social media daily and consider it one of the most fundamental advancements, it doesn't mean that they don't value face-to-face interactions and quality time spent with their loved ones. When interacting with them, remember that they're more similar to you than you would ever expect, so be empathetic and appreciate what younger generations do to improve the world.

The first two chapters of this book allowed you to learn some basic information about how communication developed over the millennia and how the internet was created. In addition, you discovered step-by-step guides to set up your social media accounts, take care of your profile, and build a positive online persona that values positive social interactions and deep and strong connections. In Chapter 3, you learned how younger generations communicate through social media and the most important tools they use: slang, emojis, and laughs.

Chapter 4 showed you how attention spans are becoming shorter and how there are ways to capture them to create deeper connections with younger generations, like gamification and storytelling. In Chapter 5, you uncovered the significance of empathy and active listening and how to use these essential skills to communicate online and understand the subtleties of tone and context. When interacting with someone face-to-face, you can look at verbal and nonverbal cues that help you grasp the meaning behind their words. However, when you send a message online, you can only count on what they write to understand what they mean. To interpret messages, remember that most people don't have bad intentions and focus on the words they use to understand if they want to convey positive or negative feelings.

Chapter 6 discussed a hot topic in the online world: conflict. Arguments arise more easily on social media platforms for different reasons, the most essential ones being physical distance and platform design. People feel more free to express their opinions and criticize others harshly because they don't argue face-to-face and feel more distant. Therefore, they might easily become aggressive or offensive to protect their point of view. However, social media platform design also plays a crucial role. For example, Facebook is famous for its heated arguments because people discuss in front of their friends and feel the urge to enforce their ideas in any way to prove that they're right. In Chapter 7, you discovered the golden rules of netiquette that allow you to have positive and healthy interactions online and useful tips to keep safe while navigating the jungle of social media and websites. Finally, Chapter 8 reminded you of the importance of connecting both online and offline and taking regular breaks from the digital world to stay mentally and physically healthy.

Now, you possess all the tools you need to understand the digital landscape and communicate effectively online. Thanks to all the information you gathered in this book, you know how to connect to younger generations and create deep and strong relationships with your grandchildren both online and offline. From this moment onward, you'll feel closer to them and self-confident enough to set up your social media accounts and enter the online world. Say goodbye to missed connections and hello to a more sociable and tech-savvy you. Get your online profile started today.

# READY TO HELP YOUR GRANDCHILDREN...

Now that you are fully prepared to form deeper connections through the future of communication, and close that generation gap once and for good, you are now equipped with the power to help yourself and your grandchildren improve online relationships, reduce misunderstandings, and navigate challenging digital situations with my first book; Beyond Emojis. Never let an emoji confuse your grandchildren again! They can uncover how to communicate online in just 8 simple strategies!

**For ebook -** Click the link to get them their copy today: amazon.com/dp/B0CP9QH93Z

**For paperback -** Scan the QR Code below to get them their copy today:

# BEYOND EMOJIS

## 8 SIMPLE STRATEGIES FOR TEENS TO IMPROVE RELATIONSHIPS,

### REDUCE MISUNDERSTANDINGS, AND NAVIGATE CHALLENGING DIGITAL SITUATIONS

ALEXANDER VAUGHN

# REFERENCES

A., N. (2023, April 19). *10 essential writing strategies for effective text communication.* LinkedIn. https://www.linkedin.com/pulse/10-essential-writing-strategies-effective-text-neda-aria/

Adam12. (2023, June 27). *21 millennial slang words we're all saying now.* 105-7 Wror. https://wror.com/listicle/21-millennial-slang-words-were-all-saying-now/

Alexander, A. (2014, January 13). *How to create a Facebook account.* YouTube. https://www.youtube.com/watch?v=6cbDDg7rHok

Alton, L. (2017, May 12). Phone calls, texts or email? Here's how millennials prefer to communicate. *Forbes.* https://www.forbes.com/sites/larryalton/2017/05/11/how-do-millennials-prefer-to-communicate/?sh=744c41366d6f

Angelov, M. (2022, June 18). *Why is internet safety important in 2022?* The Digital Chain. https://thedigitalchain.com/why-is-internet-safety-important/

Aroesti, R. (2019, August 13). *"Horrifyingly absurd": How did millennial comedy get so surreal?* The Guardian. https://www.theguardian.com/tv-and-radio/2019/aug/13/how-did-millennial-comedy-get-so-surreal

Baughan, A. (2021, July 8). *It's not just bad behavior – why social media design makes it hard to have constructive disagreements online.* Government Executive. https://www.govexec.com/technology/2021/07/its-not-just-bad-behavior-why-social-media-design-makes-it-hard-have-constructive-disagreements-online/183148/

Baxter, K. (2020, May 5). *How to engage the different generations through technology.* LinkedIn. https://www.linkedin.com/pulse/how-engage-different-generations-through-technology-karl-baxter/

*The benefits of intergenerational relationships.* (2020, July 24). IRT. https://www.irt.org.au/the-good-life/the-benefits-of-intergenerational-relationships/

*The best team-building activities for millennial offices.* (2019, June 21). Fulcrum. https://www.fulcrumconsult.com/2019/06/21/the-best-team-building-activities-for-millennial-offices/

Bishop, S. (2023, June 4). *6 ways to stay calm and collected during a heated argument*. Mediate.com. https://mediate.com/6-ways-to-stay-calm-and-collected-during-a-heated-argument/

Borge, J., & Nicolaou, E. (2021, June 25). *Here's what all of those popular slang words really mean*. Oprah Daily. https://www.oprahdaily.com/entertainment/g23603568/slang-words-meaning/

Brisinger, A. (n.d.). *Gen Z vs baby boomers: The most common similarities and differences*. Startups Magazine. https://startupsmagazine.co.uk/article-gen-z-vs-baby-boomers-most-common-similarities-and-differences

Burton, M. (2020, June 23). *Become a better listener with these 5 exercises from improvised comedy*. LinkedIn. https://www.linkedin.com/pulse/become-better-listener-5-exercises-from-improvised-comedy-mike-burton/

*Can you feel someone's vibe through text?* (2022, March 18). Conscious Vibe. https://theconsciousvibe.com/how-do-you-feel-someones-vibe-through-text/

Carroll, P. (2022, September 23). *7 ways to improve your online debates*. Foundation for Economic Education. https://fee.org/articles/7-ways-to-improve-your-online-debates/

Case. (2017, September 21). *Is the internet really forever?* LearnSafe. https://learnsafe.com/is-the-internet-really-forever/

Cherry, K. (2020, November 19). *How to do a digital detox*. Verywell Mind. https://www.verywellmind.com/why-and-how-to-do-a-digital-detox-4771321

Cherry, K. (2023, February 22). *What is empathy?* Verywell Mind. https://www.verywellmind.com/what-is-empathy-2795562

Cockrell, M. (2022, October 19). *The power of intergenerational connection*. Generations. https://generations.asaging.org/power-intergenerational-connection

Converse Willkomm, A. (2018, October 17). *12 tips for writing effective emails*. Drexel University Graduate College. https://drexel.edu/graduatecollege/professional-development/blog/2018/October/12-tips-for-writing-effective-emails/

*Core value: Character*. (2018, August 13). Essential2Life. https://www.e2lonline.com/post/core-value-character

*Create an Instagram account*. (n.d.). Help Center | Instagram. https://help.instagram.com/155940534568753

Crestodina, A. (2018, July 3). *9 tips to nail your social media profile picture*

(*with research and examples*). Orbit Media Studios. https://www.orbit
media.com/blog/perfect-profile-pictures-9-tips-plus-some-research/

*Cyber safety tips for adults.* (2018, January 9). StaySafe.org. https://staysafe.
org/cyber-safety-tips-for-adults/

Davey, L. (2016, March 3). *When an argument gets too heated, here's what to
say.* Harvard Business Review. https://hbr.org/2016/03/when-an-argu
ment-gets-too-heated-heres-what-to-say

*Digital literacy for seniors: Exploring the benefits and challenges.* (2023,
August 23). Visavie. https://visavie.com/en/digital-literacy-for-seniors

*The different dangers of the Internet.* (n.d.). SaferWeb. https://saferweb.be/
the-different-dangers-of-the-internet/?lang=en

Ducharme, J. (2023, August 10). *Why everyone's worried about their attention span—and how to improve yours.* Time. https://time.com/
6302294/why-you-cant-focus-anymore-and-what-to-do-about-it/

*8 top digital marketing trends that will define 2024.* (2024, January 23).
Edna. https://edna.io/resources/blog-8-digital-communications-trends-
in-2024/

Enright, T. (2023, April 25). *Overcoming the generational gap: 4 impactful
realizations for recruitment & retention success.* Yoh. https://www.yoh.
com/blog/overcoming-the-generational-gap

Farrier, E. (2023, November 23). *How to check if a website is safe: An 11-
step guide.* Norton. https://us.norton.com/blog/how-to/check-if-a-
website-is-safe

*5 benefits of your online identity.* (2020, February 11). Meic. https://www.
meiccymru.org/5-benefits-of-your-online-identity/

Friedman, D. (2022, September 13). *Digital detox: Your 10-step guide.*
Health. https://www.health.com/mind-body/digital-detox

Geoffrey, M. (2022, June 26). *When you strongly disagree with someone:
How to find common ground.* Tiny Buddha. https://tinybuddha.com/
blog/when-you-strongly-disagree-with-someone-how-to-find-common-
ground/

George, K. (2017, January 31). *How to create a social media profile that is
impossible to ignore.* YourChicGeek. https://yourchicgeek.com/create-
a-social-media-profile/

Gillette, H. (2022, April 4). *How to be more empathetic.* Psych Central.
https://psychcentral.com/health/how-to-be-more-empathetic

Glukhovskyy, A. (2023, March 30). *The future of digital communication:*

*Emerging trends and opportunities.* Growth Tribe. https://growthtribe.
io/blog/digital-communication-trends

Hogarty, S. (2022, October 18). *Ways to communicate with millennials in
the workplace.* We Work Ideas. https://www.wework.com/ideas/profes
sional-development/management-leadership/ways-to-communicate-
with-millennials-in-the-workplace

Hollander, A. (2023, September 14). *Average human attention span by age:
60 statistics.* BridgeCare ABA Therapy. https://www.bridgecareaba.
com/blog/average-human-attention-span

*How can you bridge the generation gap?* (n.d.). LinkedIn. https://www.
linkedin.com/advice/0/how-can-you-bridge-generation-gap-skills-
professional-mentoring

*How can you write engaging web content for readers with short attention
spans?* (n.d.). LinkedIn. Retrieved May 15, 2024, from https://www.
linkedin.com/advice/0/how-can-you-write-engaging-web-content-read
ers-short-attention-5nwuc

*How can you write SMS messages that are clear and concise?* (n.d.).
LinkedIn. Retrieved May 8, 2024, from https://www.linkedin.com/
advice/0/how-can-you-write-sms-messages-clear-concise

*How do I create a strong and unique password?* (2004). WebRoot. https://
www.webroot.com/us/en/resources/tips-articles/how-do-i-create-a-
strong-password

*How to build your technical confidence: Strategies for older adults.* (2022,
August 17). National Council on Aging. https://www.ncoa.org/article/
how-to-build-your-technical-confidence-strategies-for-older-adults

*How to setup a Twitter account.* (n.d.). Retrieved May 6, 2024, from https://
tsta.org/sites/default/files/Twitter.pdf

Hughes, J. (2018, April 20). *10 tips to craft the perfect social media profile.*
Hootsuite.    https://blog.hootsuite.com/ways-to-improve-your-social-
media-profiles/

Ištvanović, I. (2021, October 26). *Why attention spans are short and five
useful tricks that show how online learning can improve them.* EWyse.
https://ewyse.agency/blog/why-attention-spans-are-short-and-five-
useful-tricks-that-show-how-online-learning-can-improve-them/

Jaffe, E. (2014, October 9). *Why it's so hard to detect emotion in emails and
texts.* Fast Company. https://www.fastcompany.com/3036748/why-its-
so-hard-to-detect-emotion-in-emails-and-texts

Jenkins, R. (2014). *How generation Z uses technology and social media.*

Ryan Jenkins. https://blog.ryan-jenkins.com/how-generation-z-uses-technology-and-social-media

Joe, C. (2023, May 4). *How to use Facebook: Everything you need to know.* Android Authority. https://www.androidauthority.com/how-to-use-facebook-3155263/

K, A. (2023, June 14). *What is a website? Understanding the components and different categories.* Hostinger Tutorials. https://www.hostinger.com/tutorials/what-is-website/

Keeley, J. (2020, August 22). *The 150 most popular emojis explained.* Make Use Of. https://www.makeuseof.com/top-emojis-explained-cheat-sheet/

Lama, D. (n.d.). *A quote by Dalai Lama.* GoodReads. https://www.goodreads.com/quotes/7062036-when-you-talk-you-are-only-repeating-what-you-already

Larbalestier, J. (2009, December 18). *Commenting etiquette.* Justine Larbalestier. https://justinelarbalestier.com/blog/2009/12/18/commenting-etiquette/

Lawler, M. (2021, December 30). *How to do a digital detox without unplugging completely.* Everyday Health. https://www.everydayhealth.com/emotional-health/how-to-do-a-digital-detox-without-unplugging-completely/

Lawson, J. (n.d.). *How to connect with your grandchildren.* Psyche. Retrieved May 14, 2024, from https://psyche.co/guides/how-to-connect-with-your-grandchildren-for-both-your-sakes

Lebow, H. I. (2016, May 17). *Become a better listener: Active listening.* Psych Central. https://psychcentral.com/lib/become-a-better-listener-active-listening

Liles, M. (2022, January 2). *50 gen Z slang words you need to know to keep from becoming "cheugy."* Parade. https://parade.com/1293898/marynliles/gen-z-slang-words/

Lindner, J. (2023, December 8). *Must-Know internet dangers statistics [latest report].* Gitnux. https://gitnux.org/internet-dangers-statistics/

Litman, R. (2024, February 15). *Harnessing the unexpected similarities of gen Z & boomers.* LinkedIn. https://www.linkedin.com/pulse/harnessing-unexpected-similarities-gen-z-boomers-reid-litman-uksfc/

Lloyd, A. (2023, August 19). *Inside "Gen Z humor," the layered and absurdist internet jokes millennials are struggling to keep up with.* Business Insider. https://www.businessinsider.com/millennials-struggling-absur

dist-gen-z-humor-memes-2023-8

*Maintaining a positive online reputation.* (n.d.). MindTools. Retrieved May 6, 2024, from https://www.mindtools.com/ayri6rb/maintaining-a-positive-online-reputation

*Managing your online identity.* (2019). The Carnegie Cyber Academy. http://www.carnegiecyberacademy.com/facultyPages/communication/identity.html

Mather, C.-J. (2022, April 27). *A brief history on the evolution of communication.* CHF beyond Communication. https://www.cfh.com/insights/blogs/communications/a-brief-history-on-the-evolution-of-communication/

Menguin, J. (2023, May 30). *Netiquette & the 10 golden rules of online interaction.* Jef Menguin. https://jefmenguin.com/netiquette-rules/

Mileva, G. (2022, March 16). *The ultimate beginner's guide to using TikTok in 2024.* Influencer Marketing Hub. https://influencermarketinghub.com/how-to-use-tiktok-beginners/

*Millennials: Technology = social connection.* (2014, February). Nielsen. https://www.nielsen.com/insights/2014/millennials-technology-social-connection/

MindTools Content Team. (n.d.). *Writing effective emails.* MindTools. https://www.mindtools.com/apz815y/writing-effective-emails

Mothay, S. (2012, May 6). *How to deal with generation gap.* WisdomTimes. https://www.wisdomtimes.com/blog/how-to-deal-with-generation-gap/

Munoz, R. (2017, June 15). *The evolution of communication through the centuries.* MobileCon. https://www.mobilecon2012.com/the-evolution-of-communication-through-the-centuries/

My, D. (2023, September 26). *How to use linkedin for beginners.* LinkedIn. https://www.linkedin.com/pulse/how-use-linkedin-beginners-do-my/

Olsson, R. (2022, September 5). *Healthy conflict: How to recognize and handle a heated conversation.* Banner Health. https://www.bannerhealth.com/healthcareblog/advise-me/how-to-recognize-and-handle-a-heated-conversation

*Online offline interactions.* (n.d.). FasterCapital. Retrieved May 14, 2024, from https://fastercapital.com/keyword/online-offline-interactions.html

*Op-Ed: Why boomers, gen Z have more in common than either group realizes.* (2020, February 6). Money & Markets. https://moneyandmarkets.com/baby-boomers-generation-z-more-in-common/

Pasunuri, S. (2024, February 25). *Privacy etiquette: Respecting boundaries in a digital age.* LinkedIn. https://www.linkedin.com/pulse/privacy-etiquette-respecting-boundaries-digital-age-sreenu-pasunuri-ntsae/

Perry, J. (2019, August 28). *5 tips for engaging in online debate.* BioLogos. https://biologos.org/articles/5-tips-for-engaging-in-online-debate

Rai, I. (2020, June 15). *The anatomy of an online argument.* Medium. https://medium.com/@radshaan/the-anatomy-of-an-online-argument-8676d78a4c29

Rogow, M. (2023, January 5). *8 effective ways to capture the 8-second attention span in 2023.* LinkedIn. https://www.linkedin.com/pulse/8-effective-ways-capture-8-second-attention-span-2023-maury-rogow-ceo/

Sanderson, B. (n.d.). *A quote by Brandon Sanderson.* GoodReads. https://www.goodreads.com/quotes/306111-the-purpose-of-a-storyteller-is-not-to-tell-you

Saunders, E. G. (2020, October 28). *How to stop getting into pointless arguments online.* Wired. https://www.wired.com/story/how-to-stop-arguing-online/

Sean. (2018, September 30). *Thumper's rule - knowing when and how to avoid an online argument.* SocMedSean. https://www.socmedsean.com/thumpers-rule-knowing-when-and-how-to-avoid-an-online-argument/

Sernoff, L. (2022, June 8). *How to use Twitter: An A-Z starter guide.* Wix Blog. https://www.wix.com/blog/twitter-guide-for-beginners

Sharma, N. C. (2019, September 16). *Why is digital literacy important for elderly?* Mint. https://www.livemint.com/education/news/why-is-digital-literacy-important-for-elderly-1568620357404.html

Shea, M. (2018, July 13). *Assume no more: 5 questions to help you learn someone's perspective.* Shine. https://advice.theshineapp.com/articles/assume-no-more-5-questions-to-help-you-learn-someones-perspective/

*Similarities and differences between baby boomers and millennials.* (2022, October 18). BoomAgain. https://boomagain.com/similarities-and-differences-between-baby-boomers-and-millennials/

Singh, P. (2023, March 9). *Online communication – A complete guide.* REVE Chat. https://www.revechat.com/blog/online-communication/

Singh, R. (2022, March 16). *Emoji meanings: Types of emojis and what do they mean.* 91mobiles. https://www.91mobiles.com/hub/emoji-meanings/

*6 quick tips for writing effective emails.* (2016, November 9). Grammarly. https://www.grammarly.com/blog/how-to-write-effective-emails/

*Social media etiquette 101: The dos and don'ts of posting on social media.* (2023, October 5). Social Hospitality. https://socialhospitality.com/2023/10/social-media-etiquette-101-the-dos-and-donts-of-posting-on-social-media/

Sombret, P. (2023, July 27). *Gen Z communication style: How to grasp the generation with the briefest attention span.* DeskBird. https://www.deskbird.com/blog/generation-z-communication-preferences

Stedman, A. (2019, April 9). *A quick guide to Instagram DM etiquette.* The Frugality. https://the-frugality.com/a-guide-to-instagram-dm-etiquette/

Stone, R. (2021, February 27). *How arguing with strangers on the internet affects your mental health.* YourTango. https://www.yourtango.com/experts/rachelle-stone/how-arguing-strangers-internet-affects-your-mental-health

Streets, M. (2023, September 11). *The history of emoji.* TechTarget. https://www.techtarget.com/whatis/feature/The-history-of-emoji

Su, A. J. (2016, June 9). *3 ways to stay calm when conversations get intense.* Harvard Business Review. https://hbr.org/2016/06/3-ways-to-stay-calm-when-conversations-get-intense

Tartakovsky, M. (2016, May 17). *10 tips for setting boundaries online.* Psych Central. https://psychcentral.com/lib/10-tips-for-setting-boundaries-online#1

*These are gen Z's 15 biggest hobbies.* (2022, May 18). YPulse. https://www.ypulse.com/article/2022/05/18/these-are-gen-zs-15-biggest-hobbies/?pi_list_email=pamela.arienti96%40gmail.com

*3 reasons people argue online? And here's why it's useless!* (2020, September 8). The Thinking Bat Newsletter. https://thinkingbat.substack.com/p/3-reasons-people-argue-online-and

Thu-Huong, H. (2021, March 16). *5 exercises to help you build more empathy.* Ideas.ted.com. https://ideas.ted.com/5-exercises-to-help-you-build-more-empathy/

*Tips for helping seniors embrace technology.* (n.d.). PACE of Southwest Michigan. Retrieved May 2, 2024, from https://www.paceswmi.org/paceblog/seniors-technology-tips

*Tips for improving your email writing skills (with examples).* (2021, August 24). LightKey. https://www.lightkey.io/post/email-writing-skills

*Top 10 internet safety rules & what not to do online.* (2020). Kaspersky. https://www.kaspersky.com/resource-center/preemptive-safety/top-10-preemptive-safety-rules-and-what-not-to-do-online

*The top 10 things gen Z & millennials are doing in their free time.* (2022, June 7). YPulse. https://www.ypulse.com/article/2022/06/07/the-top-10-things-gen-z-millennials-are-doing-in-their-free-time/?pi_list_email=pamela.arienti96%40gmail.com

*Top 50 interesting facts about social media to blow your mind.* (2022, September 8). Skyram. https://www.skyramtechnologies.com/blog/top-50-interesting-facts-about-social-media-to-blow-your-mind/

*The 2024 social media demographics guide.* (2024). Khoros. https://khoros.com/resources/social-media-demographics-guide

*200+ emojis explained: Types of emojis, what do they mean & how to use them.* (2022, May 28). Smartprix. https://www.smartprix.com/bytes/a-guide-to-emojis-types-of-emojis-what-do-they-mean-how-to-use-them/

Uenuma, F. (2020, May 11). *Video chat is helping us stay connected in lockdown. But the tech was once a "spectacular flop."* Time. https://time.com/5834516/video-chat-zoom-history/

*Understanding others: The importance of perspective taking.* (2023, August 21). Everyday Speech. https://everydayspeech.com/sel-implementation/understanding-others-the-importance-of-perspective-taking/

V., V. (2022, January 22). *How to set up LinkedIn profile step by step (easy & in-depth tutorial).* YouTube. https://www.youtube.com/watch?v=SzeG_FplOPo

Ven, N. (2023, November 5). *How to create a TikTok account? Step by step tutorial.* YouTube. https://www.youtube.com/watch?v=wmHeaSqs3lE

*What are some effective ways to use humor in your communication with clients and colleagues?* (2023, March 9). *LinkedIn.* https://www.linkedin.com/advice/0/what-some-effective-ways-use-humor-your-communication

*What is a website?* (2021, July 5). GeeksforGeeks. https://www.geeksforgeeks.org/what-is-a-website/

Wooll, M. (2021, August 25). *Finding common ground with anyone: A quick and easy guide.* BetterUp. https://www.betterup.com/blog/finding-common-ground-with-anyone-a-quick-and-easy-guide

Yarnell, K. (n.d.). *8 ways to reach gen Z with technology.* Tithe.ly. https://get.tithe.ly/blog/8-ways-to-reach-gen-z-with-technology

Zalani, R. (2017, November 1). *Instagram 101: A step-by-step guide on how to use instagram.* Buffer. https://buffer.com/library/how-to-use-instagram/

Zetlin, M. (2015, November 25). *11 phrases that will help you defuse an argument.* Inc. https://www.inc.com/minda-zetlin/11-phrases-that-will-help-you-defuse-an-argument.html

Zhu, N. (2022, November 16). *Internet 101: A complete guide and explanation to the internet.* Internxt. https://blog.internxt.com/internet-complete-guide/

## IMAGE REFERENCES

Burton, K. (2020). *Multiracial positive male and female students using smartphones in city park* [Image]. Pexels. https://www.pexels.com/photo/multiracial-positive-male-and-female-students-using-smart phones-in-city-park-6146931/

*Chat communication connection.* (2021). [Image]. Pixabay. https://pixabay.com/photos/chat-communication-connection-6565447/

Choudhary, S. (2019). *Man holding laptop computer with both hands* [Image]. Pexels. https://www.pexels.com/photo/man-holding-laptop-computer-with-both-hands-2036656/

*Computer monitor users edit desk.* (2015). [Image]. Pixabay. https://pixabay.com/photos/computer-monitor-users-edit-desk-663046/

Cottonbro Studio. (2020). *A group of students standing in the gym while holding placards* [Image]. Pexels. https://www.pexels.com/photo/a-group-of-students-standing-in-the-gym-while-holding-placards-6217820/

Daboul, S. (2018). *Close-up photography of smartphone* [Image]. Pexels. https://www.pexels.com/photo/close-up-photography-of-smartphone-1035103/

Elliott, T. (2020). *Photo of person using black laptop* [Image]. Pexels. https://www.pexels.com/photo/photo-of-person-using-black-laptop-4112363/

Kampus Production. (2021). *People playing chess on table* [Image]. Pexels. https://www.pexels.com/photo/people-playing-chess-on-table-7799562/

Negative Space. (2016). *Black and gray macbook computer keyboard* [Image]. Pexels. https://www.pexels.com/photo/working-macbook-computer-keyboard-34577/

Pandit, R. (2019). *Blue and red light from computer* [Image]. Pexels. https://www.pexels.com/photo/blue-and-red-light-from-computer-1933900/

Piacqaudio, A. (n.d.). *Pensive grandmother with granddaughter having interesting conversation while cooking together in light modern kitchen*

[Image]. Pexels. https://www.pexels.com/photo/pensive-grandmother-with-granddaughter-having-interesting-conversation-while-cooking-together-in-light-modern-kitchen-3768146/

Piacquadio, A. (2020). *Young troubled woman using laptop at home* [Image]. Pexels. https://www.pexels.com/photo/young-troubled-woman-using-laptop-at-home-3755755/

Pinwhalestock. (2019). *Emojis hipster funny* [Image]. Pixabay. https://pixabay.com/vectors/emojis-emoji-hipster-funny-4518355/

Pixabay. (2016). *Close-up photography of smartphone icons* [Image]. Pexels. https://www.pexels.com/photo/close-up-photography-of-smartphone-icons-267350/

Shimazaki, S. (2020). *Crop faceless person using laptop and smartphone in darkness* [Image]. Pexels. https://www.pexels.com/photo/crop-faceless-person-using-laptop-and-smartphone-in-darkness-5926383/

Shvets Production. (2021). *Man in black suit jacket holding smartphone* [Image]. Pexels. https://www.pexels.com/photo/man-in-black-suit-jacket-holding-smartphone-8899568/

Subiyanto, K. (2020). *Girlfriends working with interest in collaborative project* [Image]. Pexels. https://www.pexels.com/photo/girlfriends-working-with-interest-on-collaborative-project-4126753/

Tankilevitch, P. (2021a). *Three young women posing together* [Image]. Pexels. https://www.pexels.com/photo/tree-young-women-posing-together-6988597/

Tankilevitch, P. (2021b). *Woman holding a black camera* [Image]. Pexels. https://www.pexels.com/photo/woman-holding-a-black-camera-6988608/

TheDigitalArtist. (2017). *Earth internet globalization* [Image]. Pixabay. https://pixabay.com/photos/earth-internet-globalization-2254769/

"35 Quotes About Communication to Inspire Collaboration." Vibe: All-in-One Smart Whiteboard for Collaborative Workspace. Last modified May 5, 2022. https://vibe.us/blog/35-quotes-about-communication/?srsltid=AfmBOoqkwzwdlGSn4eFxpu_cvFZJ6JjVYo_-R-VOQhAdlPkcH2Sk7RLG

# ABOUT THE AUTHOR

Alexander Vaughn is a dynamic 38-year-old father of three who is ardently dedicated to his role as a communication expert and author, particularly focusing on teens in the digital age.

With an expansive background in both the tech and education sectors, Alexander is a fervent promoter of effective digital communication among teens. He believes in the balance between utilizing modern tools and ensuring that teens' communication skills are not compromised in today's technology-driven world.

He commits himself to crafting guides and resources that are both engaging and practical, ensuring that today's youth are well-equipped to express themselves confidently and safely online. Drawing from his extensive research and hands-on experience, Alexander has now authored his second book addressing the nuances of communication in the digital era.

Alexander's vision is to bridge the communication gap between generations, making sure that every teen is not just tech-savvy but also communication proficient. He aspires to touch the lives of countless young individuals, emphasizing that authentic and effective communication is just as crucial in the digital realm as it is offline.

His dedication and enthusiasm for nurturing effective digital communicators resonate deeply, making his books an essential companion for teens, parents, and grandparents navigating the online world.